Volleyball

STEPS TO SUCCESS

Becky Schmidt

HUMAN KINETICS

Library of Congress Cataloging-in-Publication Data

Schmidt, Becky, 1976-
  Volleyball : steps to success / Becky Schmidt.
      pages cm
  1. Volleyball. 2. Volleyball--Coaching. 3. Volleyball--Officiating. I. Title.
  GV1015.3.S35 2015
  796.32507'7--dc23
                                                     2015015891
ISBN: 978-1-4504-6882-4 (print)

The web addresses cited in this text were current as of June 2015, unless otherwise noted.

Acquisitions Editor: Justin Klug

Developmental Editor: Cynthia McEntire

Managing Editor: Nicole Moore

Copyeditor: Annette Pierce

Senior Graphic Designer: Keri Evans

Cover Designer: Keith Blomberg

Photograph (cover): Matt Brown/iStock

Photographs (interior): Neil Bernstein

Visual Production Assistant: Joyce Brumfield

Photo Production Manager: Jason Allen

Art Manager: Kelly Hendren

Associate Art Manager: Alan L. Wilborn

Illustrations: © Human Kinetics

Printer: Walsworth

We thank Hope College in Holland, Michigan, for assistance in providing the location for the photo shoot for this book.

Printed in the United States of America   10 9 8 7 6 5 4 3 2 1

The paper in this book was manufactured using responsible forestry methods.

Human Kinetics
Website: www.HumanKinetics.com

United States: Human Kinetics
P.O. Box 5076
Champaign, IL 61825-5076
800-747-4457
e-mail: humank@hkusa.com

Canada: Human Kinetics
475 Devonshire Road Unit 100
Windsor, ON N8Y 2L5
800-465-7301 (in Canada only)
e-mail: info@hkcanada.com

Europe: Human Kinetics
107 Bradford Road
Stanningley
Leeds LS28 6AT, United Kingdom
+44 (0) 113 255 5665
e-mail: hk@hkeurope.com

Australia: Human Kinetics
57A Price Avenue
Lower Mitcham, South Australia 5062
08 8372 0999
e-mail: info@hkaustralia.com

New Zealand: Human Kinetics
P.O. Box 80
Mitcham Shopping Centre, South Australia 5062
0800 222 062
e-mail: info@hknewzealand.com

E6146

Volleyball

STEPS TO SUCCESS

Contents

Climbing the Steps to Volleyball Success

Like many others, the foundation of my volleyball success staircase began in an elementary gym class. We started out playing with balloons instead of balls and graduated quickly to full-court volleyball played at a net height for adults. Truth be told, I didn't like it very much since there seemed to be more standing around than action. When a friend asked me to try out for the team in middle school, I complied only because I liked the people who were playing. In fact, my love of the game itself didn't develop until college when I was able to gain enough skill to control the ball and not just have it rebound randomly around the court. It took time to learn how to read the opponent and anticipate where she planned to attack. It took creativity to develop tactics that put our team into better positions to be successful. It took patience to learn how to set up a game plan and to understand that it sometimes takes losing a point to win a match. None of this happened overnight and it won't for you either, but if you persevere and continue to climb the staircase of success, I think you might fall in love with this game as I have.

Despite the challenges of learning this game, volleyball is incredibly popular the world over. It is played by nearly 50 million Americans and is one of the big five international sports. The Fédération Internationale de Volleyball (FIVB) is the largest international sporting federation in the world with 220 national governing bodies. On August 30, 2014, more than 61,500 spectators watched the Polish men's national team beat Serbia in the opening round of the World Championships at the Warsaw National Stadium (typically a soccer venue). More than 300,000 adults and juniors compete in USA Volleyball events each year on indoor, sand, and grass courts.

While you may not have the desire to become an All-American athlete or coach a team to a national championship, the volleyball staircase of success looks different for every participant. It may be as simple as learning how to get your serve over the net or as challenging as coaching a youth team to a tournament championship. Maybe you are trying to win an intramural championship, pick up a new hobby, make new friends, or make a comeback to a game that has seen changes since you last played. Regardless of your motivations, success is not far away.

In *Volleyball: Steps to Success*, you will learn key components of volleyball's fundamental skills as well as how to practice them. Every effort has been made to help you understand why performing skills a specific way is valuable. As you work through each of the skill elements, follow this sequence to maximize your learning:

1. Study the skill covered in each step, why it is important, and how to perform it.

2. Observe the photos of demonstrators modeling how to perform the techniques successfully.

3. Read and practice each drill and track your progress in each of the success checks at the end of the skill element chapters.

4. Have a qualified observer, such as your teacher, coach, or a trained peer, evaluate your skills after completing each set of drills and compare their assessment of your skill to your own.

5. Once you have achieved the indicated level of success in each skill element, you can move on to the next step.

While you may be anxious to move through the steps quickly, be sure to revisit skill elements to keep your game strong. You can always increase the challenge of each drill (or reduce it if you are struggling) by adjusting the pace, length, complexity, or standards involved. Specific positions will require more training in individual skills, but volleyball players should be able to perform all of the skills to a certain degree. Continue to practice the basics so that you are versatile and able to be your best when the game is on the line.

Of course, the ultimate test is playing the game itself, and it is also the most fun. When playing volleyball before getting through all of the steps, make sure to keep your focus on the step you are currently working on. Try not to get distracted by aspects of the game that you have not yet learned or you will take more steps backward than forward. By taking the time to practice each element in a controlled setting and then bringing that learning to the context of a competitive game, you will see your skills improve and your understanding of the game grow. Throughout your experience with this great game, do not be afraid to fail, try to mimic those who perform the skills well, envision yourself being successful, practice often and deliberately, and trust the process. I wish you all the best and many long rallies!

Acknowledgments

The number of mentors and friends who have influenced my work are too numerous to list. A few from my time at Hope College, Miami University, and the University of Redlands include Maureen Dunn, Karla Wolters, Carolyn Condit, Lisa Dankovich, Paco Labrador, and Suzette Soboti. I am also grateful to the American Volleyball Coaches Association (AVCA) for inspiring the free exchange of ideas among coaches from every division of volleyball across the continent.

I have had the distinct pleasure to work with many extraordinary student-athletes. I am deeply grateful for the impact that they have had on our program and proud of the women they have become. I am especially proud of those who have chosen to pursue coaching as a way to give back to their sport. My dedicated assistant coaches deserve thanks as well, especially Jean Kegerreis, who has been a loyal and selfless partner in the annual quest for team success.

Teaching and coaching are difficult jobs. I would not have been able to devote so much time and effort to my student-athletes without the support of my husband, Dave Fleece, and my parents, Boyd and Sara Wilson and John Schmidt and Dawn Boelkins. Thanks for loving not just me, but my student-athletes as well.

The Sport of Volleyball

"Volley Ball is a new game which is pre-eminently fitted for the gymnasium or the exercise hall, but which may also be played out-of-doors. Any number of persons may play the game. The play consists of keeping a ball in motion over a high net, from one side to the other, thus partaking of the character of two games—tennis and hand ball."

Original rules of volleyball from *Official Handbook of the Young Men's Christian Associations of North America* (www.volleyball.org/rules/rules_1897.html)

Volleyball has changed a great deal since William Morgan first invented the game in a YMCA gymnasium more than 100 years ago. However, as you can see from the first line of his rulebook, the spirit of the game has remained the same. Morgan's visionary flexibility in the number of participants and acceptable venues for the sport has resulted in incredible participatory popularity. From backyard grass courts to sand volleyball Olympic venues and major arenas, volleyball is one of the most popular sports in the world. In the United States alone, 6.6 million men and women play volleyball annually.

HISTORY

William Morgan, director of physical education at the YMCA in Holyoke, Massachusetts, invented volleyball in the winter of 1895 as a less rough alternative to basketball that still demanded the same degree of physical exertion. Volleyball had a structure similar to baseball, with the game being played over nine innings and points scored only by the serving team. An inning consisted of one team serving to the other until the serving side lost three rallies (called outs) followed by the opposing team doing the same. Both teams then rotated and a new inning began. The court was marginally smaller than modern courts (25 feet [7.6 m] square on each side of the net instead of the current 29 feet, 6 inches [9 m]) and the net height was 6 feet, 6 inches (2 m) from the floor. The ball was batted from one player to another and from one side to another without the ball coming to a visible rest. Doing so resulted in an illegal contact and loss of rally, which is a similar violation as in volleyball played today.

Several differences exist between Morgan's volleyball and the modern game. First, players were allowed to dribble the ball anywhere on the court beyond the dribble line (a line running 4 feet [1.2 m] from the net) as a method of controlling it on their side. Players were allowed as many contacts as they wished before sending the ball to the opposing court, as opposed to the three contacts current players are allowed. The server was allowed a second serve if he missed the first attempt as in tennis. Any ball striking the net, except on the first service, was deemed illegal and resulted in the loss of rally for the last team that touched it. Any ball striking the line was considered out of play, while in today's game, the line is considered in play. You can read all of the original 1897 rules at www.archive.org/details/officialhandbook00athl through their website.

Volleyball grew in popularity through the widespread influence of the YMCA as well as through affiliated physical education programs at Springfield College (Massachusetts) and George Williams College (Illinois). The YMCA's international connections took the game to Canada, the Philippines, China, Japan, Burma, and India. Later, volleyball found its way to South America and Europe. According to the Fédération Internationale de Volleyball (FIVB), in 1916, an estimated 200,000 people were playing volleyball in the United States, and the National Collegiate Athletic Association instituted its first volleyball rulebook for intercollegiate competition.

After being demonstrated in an American sports exposure event at the 1924 Paris Olympic Games, the international interest in volleyball continued to grow until it was added as an Olympic sport to the Tokyo Games in 1964. Despite its invention in the United States, other countries dominated global competitions and in the women's competition that year, Japan took advantage of its home court and won the gold over the Soviet Union. The Soviet Union won gold in the men's tournament, however, beating Czechoslovakia. The most indoor volleyball Olympic medals across both sexes belongs to the Soviet Union with 12, a number that climbs to 18 when Russian medals are included after 1996. Japan and Brazil are the next closest with nine. The United States has won three Olympic gold medals in men's indoor volleyball (1984, 1988, and 2008), while the women's team has won three silver indoor volleyball medals (1984, 2008, and 2012).

While most participants compete in indoor volleyball, 4.4 million Americans also competed in sand volleyball. In 1992, beach volleyball was a demonstrated sport at the Barcelona Summer Olympic Games and officially added to the roster of Olympic sports in 1996. In contrast to indoor volleyball, sand volleyball was invented in southern California and continues to showcase the sport's top talent. American volleyball legend Karch Kiraly, with his teammate Kent Steffes, added a beach volleyball gold medal to the previous two he had won with the men's indoor team in 1984 and 1988. In the London Games of 2012, Misty May-Treanor and Kerri Walsh won their third consecutive gold medal in beach volleyball.

Grass tournaments and leagues have led to a variety of tournament formats, themes, and venues. The flexibility of Morgan's original rules regarding the number of players and the venue has facilitated volleyball's growth. Tournaments and leagues can be found for mud, snow, pavement, or water volleyball and for teams of two through nine participants. Sitting volleyball is the established Paralympic version of the sport in which athletes with lower-extremity disabilities can compete on a lower net and smaller court. The ways volleyball can be played is limited only by imagination, and many fun alternatives have been invented.

RULES

The rules that we are going to use most in this book are those adopted by the National Collegiate Athletic Association (NCAA) and the National Federation of State High School Associations (NFHS). There are some subtle differences between the international game or those used in recreation departments. Volleyball rules have changed significantly in the last 20 years and it is expected that they will continue to change as volleyball grows as a sport popular with spectators and television advertisers. Before competing in a match, it is wise to identify what organization's rulebook is governing the match.

Court Dimensions and Net Height

The standard volleyball court is composed of two squares 29 feet, 6 inches × 29 feet, 6 inches (9 m) divided by a net (figure 1). In men's volleyball, the net height is 7 feet, 11 5/8 inches (2.43 m), and in women's volleyball the net height is 7 feet, 4 1/8 inches (2.24 m). Antennae are attached to the net to mark the outside edges of the sidelines at the net. Any ball that contacts the net outside of the antenna or goes outside or over the antenna as it is played to the other court is illegal and indicates a loss of the rally. Both sides of the net have an attacking line that runs the width of the court 10 feet (3 m) from the net. Back-row players are not allowed to contact the ball higher than the net to attack or block balls in front of the attack line. All serves must be made with the player making contact between the two hash marks extending past the sidelines at the end line. A referee stand is attached to the stanchion on the pole farthest from the team bench area and scorers' table. Both of the poles and the referee stand should be covered in protective padding. It is also recommended that 10 feet (3 m) of free space beyond each sideline and end line be made available to ensure the safety of players running after errant balls.

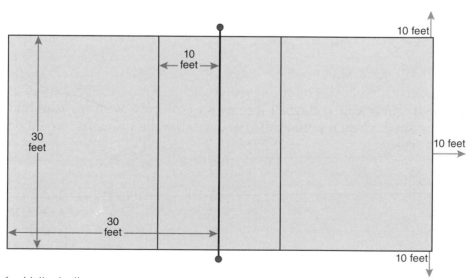

Figure 1 Volleyball court.

Scoring

Until 1998, most volleyball matches were played using side-out scoring in which the serving team was the only team eligible to score points. The length of a match was unpredictable, and matches were rarely broadcast on television because of scheduling difficulties. To make the game more appealing to television producers, the Fédération Internationale de Volleyball made the move to rally scoring in which a point is given to the team that wins the rally regardless of serve. A match is completed when one team wins three out of five or two out of three sets. A set is completed when one team reaches 25 points and has a 2-point lead, except in a match deciding the final set (the third or fifth), when the set is played to 15 points. If a team is not able to establish a 2-point lead when it reaches 25 points (or 15 points in the final set), play continues until a team can gain a 2-point lead. Seldom is a scoring cap enforced and the set can continue ad infinitum until the proper separation is achieved. Most two-of-three-set matches last from 45 minutes to an hour; a typical three-of-five-set match may last 90 minutes to two hours.

Team Members, Lineup, and Substitutions

A standard indoor volleyball match is played with six players on the court who are designated by serving order. The server is the player located in the right back. Players rotate clockwise every time a team wins the serve from its opponent and must maintain the order in which it started the match (figure 2). Players must be in service order when the ball is served by either side, but once the ball is in play they can move to any position on the court. Playing rules prevent back-row players from attacking or blocking balls above the height of the net in front of the attack line, so it is best if back-row players remain in the back row while the rally is played. Substitutions are allowed; however, once a substitution is made, that player is limited to playing in the same position in the serving order for the duration of the set. Players are allowed to reenter the game as often as they choose, but most rules limit a team to 12 or 15 total substitutions each set.

While the official rules of volleyball require six players, the game can be played with any number less than that. As long as both sides are equal, you can play 5v5, 4v4, or even 1v1, with each player getting to make three contacts in a row. Clearly establish the rules before play and have fun with the variations.

PLAYER POSITIONS

Many competitive teams use specialized positions that focus on specific skills, while recreational teams require every player to perform every skill. Specialization can result in a higher level of play, but can also be confusing for beginners. You should explore every position and the responsibilities associated with them before attempting to specialize. The specific positions will be described in greater detail in step 9, but a brief introduction will help you understand many skills along the way.

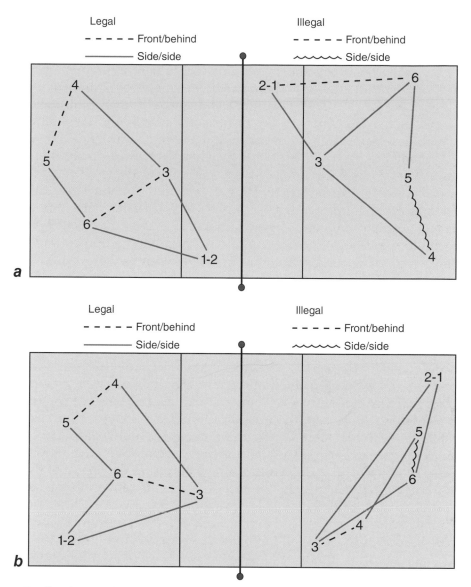

Figure 2 Service and overlaps.

Left-Side, Right-Side, and Middle Hitters

The left-side hitter attacks and plays defense out of the left-front position (zone 4). The middle hitter attacks and blocks in the middle of the front row (zone 3). The middle hitter is primarily responsible for hitting quick sets that hold the opponent's middle blocker and closing blocks at the antennae. The right-side hitter attacks and plays defense in the right-front position (zone 2). Typically, right-side hitters are strong blockers and, because of their angle of approach, can benefit from being left-handed. Setters generally play defense from the right front when they are in the front row and right back when they are in the back row. These are the standard positions most volleyball teams use in the modern game.

Libero

The libero (pronounced lib-AIR-o) is a defensive position that was introduced to the game in 1998 in an effort to reduce the advantage of attackers and increase the duration of rallies. Typically, the libero is played by a team's best defender and passer. The libero doesn't operate under the same substitution requirements of the other players. She can exchange with players as often as she chooses without counting against the designated substitution maximum. So that the libero can be easily identified, she must wear a uniform top that clearly contrasts from the other members of the team. The libero also can replace any back-row player regardless of where that player is in the serving order. She can serve for one player and can only do so when that player's designated time in the serving order comes up. To ensure that this player focuses on playing defense, she is not allowed to hand set the ball in front of the attack line, nor can she attack a ball above the height of the net (neither in front nor behind the attacking line).

Setter

The setter is usually responsible for making the second of the team's three contacts on the ball and determines which hitter will attack the opponent. The setter often switches to play defense in the right-front and right-back position in order to facilitate getting to the typical target location just right of center and near the net. It helps when the setter is quick and has a strong understanding of the game in order to anticipate what is happening and make decisions that put her team in a position to be successful.

PLAYING THE BALL

Volleyball, above all else, is a rebound team sport. The ball must never come to a visible rest while being played. When a ball is caught or thrown or when contact with the ball is longer than an instant, the contact is illegal and results in a point for the opponent. It is also a team game and a single player cannot contact the ball two times in a row. The only time a double contact is allowed is when playing the ball from a serve or an attack and the attempt is a single move to the ball. At no time can a player make an attempt to play a ball, make contact, and then make a successive contact through another attempt. If during the course of a single attempt to play a served or attacked ball the passer makes contact with her arms and then her shoulder, the double contact is allowed.

Only front-row players are allowed to attack the ball over the net in front of the attack line. For a back-row player to attack the ball, he or she must jump from behind the attacking line before playing the ball. Landing in front of the attacking line is legal. When blocking, players may contact the ball only when a portion of the ball has entered airspace over the net or on their side, unless the opponent has used all three of their contacts. For instance, a blocker cannot reach across the net and disrupt an opponent's set unless the ball has crossed into the plane above the net. However, if the opponent has used all three contacts and the ball has not yet reached the plane, a blocker may reach into the opponent's court and contact the ball. Touching the ball on the block does not count as one of the available three contacts each side is allowed. It is illegal to attack or block a serve. Simultaneous contact between two players is counted as only one contact.

END OF RALLY

A rally ends and a point is awarded when one of the following occurs:

- The serve does not cross the net or lands out of bounds without touching a receiving player.
- A team is out of rotation when the ball is served.
- A ball is terminated to the floor.
- A ball cannot be returned by a team after touching one of the players.
- A team uses four distinct contacts (not including a block touch).
- A team commits a ball-handling or protocol violation.
- A team contacts the net while playing the ball (unless the force of the ball contacting the net forces it into the offending player).
- A player crosses over the center line completely (within the antennae) or interferes with the opponent's ability to play the ball.

In rally scoring, a point is scored at the end of each of these rallies. A replay can be called in the following situations:

- Simultaneous net contacts by opposing players.
- Interference by something or someone on the playing court (typically a ball rolling on the court from an adjacent court).
- A player injury during a rally when continuing the rally would put the player's safety at risk.

A replay results in no point being scored and the last team to serve retaining that right. A point can also be scored when the first referee assigns a red card to a team or coach. Red cards can be assessed for unsportsmanlike or disruptive behavior, improper substitution or time-out requests, or the use of aids considered illegal. A yellow card may be used at the referee's discretion as a warning for any of these actions as well.

CLOTHING AND EQUIPMENT

Uniform tops must be clearly numbered so that officials can easily identify serving order and track substitutions. It is not necessary for teams to wear contrasting uniform colors, but it does make it easier to identify faults at the net.

The first referee has the discretion to deem jewelry and some hard casts or braces too dangerous to wear during competition. Rings, earrings, and necklaces can get snagged on the net or contacted with the ball in a way that can cause significant injury and should not be worn. Hard casts worn on hands and arms can cause injury to others when playing the ball at the net. Ankle bracing and soft-sided braces on other extremities are typically allowed and safe for play.

Knee pads typically are worn by volleyball players to make diving to the floor more comfortable but are not required. In fact, when a player uses proper diving technique, knee pads are not necessary, and often players at the highest levels do not wear them.

Any athletic shoe with a nonmarking sole is acceptable for playing volleyball. Volleyball-specific shoes should keep your feet cool, minimize the vertical and lateral forces from volleyball movements, and provide stability and traction.

WARM-UP

A dynamic warm-up is recommended prior to beginning any exercise program and volleyball is no different. Gradually increasing the intensity of movement from light (e.g. jogging in place and arm circles) to moderate (e.g. driving the knees up and down and throwing the ball with a partner) will help to increase blood flow and prepare muscles and joints for activity. Since volleyball is a strenuous sport on the shoulder, it is advisable to devote a little extra time to this important joint. Working with a partner, toss the ball to yourself and attack it to your partner's feet, gradually increasing the force and speed of your arm swing. You can finish your warm-up with some light stretching.

RULE DIFFERENCES ACROSS DISCIPLINES

When William Morgan wrote the original rules of volleyball, he opened the door to many variations. Indeed, these variations have proven to be quite popular. In step 10, you will learn more details about the many variations of volleyball, but to get you playing early, the following paragraphs describe just a few recreational variations of volleyball.

Sand Volleyball (Doubles)

There is no center line, and violations are called only when interference is committed by a player. If antennae are not used, then the ball must pass between the net poles. Each set is played to 21 points, with teams switching sides every 7 points. A block touch is considered one of the team's three contacts. Players may use their hands to pass a serve only if their hands remain firm and simply deflect the ball. The court is 26 feet, 3 inches 52 × feet, 6 inches (8 m 16 × m) (3 feet [1 m] shorter and 3 feet narrower than an indoor court). A sand volleyball is slightly larger and heavier than an indoor ball so that it is less reactive to wind.

International (FIVB)

The international game limits the number of substitutions to six each set. The libero cannot serve. Net violations are illegal only at the top 3 inches (7.6 cm) of the net.

Coed

This game is played with the net at the men's height. When a team uses three contacts, at least one of the contacts must be made by a female player.

Reverse Coed

This game is played with the net at the women's height. All attacks by male players must be taken from behind the attack line.

OFFICIATING

The officiating crew includes the first referee, second referee, line judges, and the scoring table. While it is possible to play volleyball without an officiating crew, officials that take their responsibilities seriously can positively influence pace of the game and the fairness of the outcome.

The first referee is the lead official and she executes her responsibilities from an elevated stand located at the net opposite the team bench and scorer's table. Before the match, the first referee examines all equipment to ensure it meets competition standards, discusses with team representatives match expectations and changes, and organizes the warm-up protocols agreed to by each team. During the match, the first referee blows her whistle to authorize serve, signal rotation, and ball-handling and net violations (at the top of the net only). It is her decision, with help from the second referee and the line judges, whether balls land in or out of bounds and which team was the last to touch the ball in play. The first referee sanctions all misconduct and team delay penalties, signals for time-outs and substitutions, and can suspend play if the crowd becomes too disruptive. Figures 3 and 4 show the most common hand signals officials and line judges use during a volleyball match.

The second referee is located at the net pole closest to the scorer's table and team benches and is primarily responsible for ensuring that protocols are followed. The second referee is responsible for ensuring the score is accurate, checking serving order and rotational alignments of the receiving team, and identifying center-line and net violations. The second referee can assist the first referee in ball-handling violations and block touches but should never blow his whistle except for the situations that are clearly under his purview. On occasion, the first referee will ask the second referee to confer over a call, but it is always the first referee's responsibility to make judgment calls.

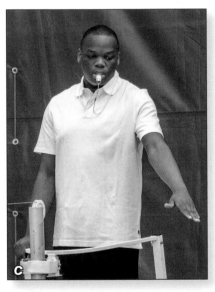

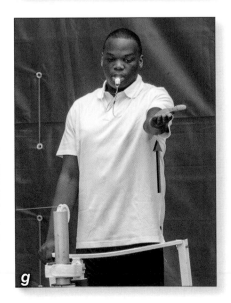

Figure 3 Officials' hand signals: *(a)* point, *(b)* serve, *(c)* in bounds, *(d)* out of bounds, *(e)* touch, *(f)* double contact, *(g)* lift, *(h)* back-row attack, *(i)* net violation *(j)* out of rotation, *(k)* center-line violation.

MISSTEP

Speaking with the officials unless you are the designated speaking captain for your team.

CORRECTION

All communication between coaches and officials happens through the speaking captain on the floor. Designated by the head coach at the start of each set, this person acts as a liaison between the first official and the coach.

Line judges are positioned in opposite corners of the court so that they can see their sideline on both sides of the net and the end line on their side of the net. Line judges must keep a steady eye on the play because they are asked to make calls on balls hit in or out and asked to call block touches and balls that cross the net over or outside of the antenna. Line judges are encouraged to move away from their positions at the corners of the court in order to get a better angle to make a call or to avoid interfering with play when in the way of a player pursuing an errant ball or a player serving from that corner. It is important to realize that while line-judging duties are often executed by other players or even parents, these people are a part of the officiating crew and are expected to pay the same attention as the referees.

Figure 4 Line judges' hand signals: *(a)* touch, *(b)* foot fault, *(c)* in, *(d)* out, *(e)* out at the antenna.

Usually three people are at the scoring table, each with specific duties. The official scorer is charged with using a paper form to make sure that all points are accounted for in the proper rotation, identify the correct server for each team, track the substitutions made, and record the number of remaining timeouts. A scoreboard operator makes sure that the visible score reflects the official scorer's score sheet. While this may seem redundant, it also ensures accuracy by having the two people agree on the score. The third person tracks the entry and exit of the libero to make sure that she is replacing the legal players and serving in the correct rotation. Statisticians, a public address announcer, and other members of the media may also be present at the scoring table.

Key to Diagrams

- - -▶	Ball path
——▶	Player movement
△	Cone
⬛	Ball cart
A	Attacker
B	Blocker
D	Digger
F	Feeder
H	Hitter
LB	Left-back player
LFB	Left-front blocker
MB	Middle-back player
MFB	Middle-front blocker
P	Passer
RB	Right-back player
RFB	Right-front blocker
S	Setter
Sv	Server
T	Target
Ts	Tosser
X, Y	Any player, when position isn't important

Serving

Every point begins with a serve. Many see it simply as the way to put the ball in play. Stronger teams see the serve as a team's first chance to put their opponent at a disadvantage. Serving effectiveness means striking a delicate balance: players must serve tough enough to force their opponent into a bad pass, but conservatively enough to avoid giving up points for serves out of bounds. To serve with accuracy and aggressiveness, players must focus on executing the skill with precision and intention.

STANDING SERVES

In volleyball, the skill that the athlete has the most control over is the standing serve. The server can control her toss, footwork, and arm swing in the way she wants to. For this reason, standing serves typically are the least prone to error; however, they still require significant coordination. This section covers the standing float and standing spin serves.

Standing Float Serve

The most common serve in volleyball is a standing float serve (figure 1.1). The server stands a few steps behind the end line, tosses the ball while stepping toward it, and strikes the center of the ball with a stiff, open palm that continues to face the target after contact. Keeping the contact point squared to the target drives the ball across the net without spin. The seams on the ball cause it to react to the air current in subtle, unpredictable ways, making it more difficult to pass (similar to a knuckleball in baseball).

To execute the standing float serve, position yourself two steps behind the end line closest to the location you have been assigned to defend. Square your feet, hips, and shoulders to the zone on the opponent's court to which you are aiming. Put your weight on the same foot as your dominant arm and the ball in your nondominant hand. Extend your nondominant arm in the direction you are aiming and cover the top of the ball with your dominant hand. Draw your dominant elbow to your ear and lightly toss the ball 2 feet (.6 m) in the air in front of your dominant shoulder. Step to the ball with the foot opposite your striking arm and contact the center of the ball with an open palm. Drive your hand through the ball, keeping your palm square to the target zone. Drive the foot on your dominant side forward and proceed to your defensive position.

Figure 1.1   STANDING FLOAT SERVE

Preparation

1. Stand two steps behind the end line close to defensive assignment.
2. Square feet, hips, and shoulders to target.
3. Put weight on foot on dominant side.
4. Hold ball in nondominant hand.
5. Extend nondominant arm to target.
6. Cover top of ball with dominant hand.

Serve

1. Draw elbow of dominant arm to ear.
2. Lightly toss ball 2 feet (6 m) up in front of dominant shoulder.
3. Step to ball with nondominant foot opposite your striking arm.
4. Contact center of ball with open palm.

Follow-Through

1. Drive hand through ball.
2. Keep palm square to target zone.
3. Drive dominant foot forward and move to defensive position.

MISSTEP

Many problems with the serve, such as the serve floating deep or wide out of bounds or into the net, stem from inaccuracy in the toss.

CORRECTION

Make sure that your toss consistently lofts the ball to space in front of your hitting shoulder. A consistent toss means a consistent contact.

Standing Spin Serve

The standing spin serve (figure 1.2) is executed with similar preparatory movements as the standing float serve, but contact with the ball involves a flexible wrist that starts lower on the ball and snaps after contact. The topspin causes the ball to travel straight and dive as the ball reaches the other side of the court. This serve is generally served harder, but because its path is more predictable, is often passed with greater accuracy than the float serve.

Position yourself two steps behind the end line closest to your defensive assignment. Square your feet, hips, and shoulders to the zone on the opponent's court to which you are aiming. Put your weight on the same foot as your dominant arm and the ball in your nondominant hand. Extend your nondominant arm in the direction to which you are aiming and cover the top of the ball with your dominant hand. Step with the foot on your nondominant side and toss the ball in front of your hitting shoulder high enough that your hitting arm will contact the lower center of the ball at full vertical reach. Throw your attacking arm to the ball so that it is maximally extended at contact. Keeping your wrist relaxed, let your hand go from a contact point on the lower position on the ball to a higher position on the ball. Follow through by letting your hitting arm fall to your hip as your foot drags behind. Proceed to your defensive position.

Figure 1.2   **STANDING SPIN SERVE**

Preparation

1. Stand two steps behind the end line close to defensive assignment.
2. Square feet, hips, and shoulders to target.
3. Put weight on foot on dominant side.
4. Hold ball in nondominant hand.
5. Extend nondominant arm to target.
6. Cover top of ball with dominant hand.
7. Step with nondominant foot.
8. Toss ball in front of hitting shoulder.

Serve

1. Throw attacking arm to ball so that arm is maximally extended at contact.
2. Keep wrist relaxed.
3. Let hand go from contact on lower position on ball to higher position on ball.

Follow-Through

1. Let hitting arm fall to hip.
2. Drag foot behind.
3. Move to defensive position.

If you contact the ball too high, you will serve the ball into the net. If you contact the ball too low, you will lob the ball out of bounds. Experiment with contacting the position on the ball that allows you to consistently serve in bounds. It is different for every player, but once you find it, try to contact the ball in the same position every time.

MISSTEP

Many players have elaborate pre-serve routines, take multiple steps to the ball, or toss the ball too high.

CORRECTION

The more movement, the greater the opportunity for error. Keeping your serve as simple as possible makes it easier to achieve consistency.

JUMP SERVES

The standing serves provide the server the greatest degree of control; jump serves bring more power. The momentum generated through the preparation phase is transferred to the ball and can increase the speed of the serve by 20 miles per hour (32 km/h) or more, but with the added power comes increased risk. The jump serve also provides an advantage in trajectory. The contact point of the jump serve is higher than that of a standing serve, which allows the path of the ball across the net to be more flat than arched. Making this trajectory as direct as possible also increases the risk of serving into the net. Fans of volleyball know that at higher levels, this risk is acceptable because of highly effective offenses when the pass is on target. Teams have to serve tough to prevent their opponents from passing well. Serving tough sometimes means accepting a higher level of risk, and jump serves might be your way to advance to a tougher serve.

Jump Float Serve

The jump float serve (figure 1.3) is the most effective serve in volleyball. The server tosses the ball a little higher and in front of herself, jumps to make contact with the ball, and keeps her wrist stiff and her palm facing the target even after contact. The higher contact point and increased speed of the ball as it travels through the air results in more movement and more challenging angles for the opponent to pass with accuracy.

Position yourself three or four steps behind the end line close to your defensive assignment. Square your feet, hips, and shoulders to the zone in the opponent's court to which you are aiming. Put your weight on the same foot as your dominant arm and the ball in your nondominant hand. Take a step and toss the ball forward and in front of the hitting shoulder. Jump forward off one foot but land on two feet as you pull both arms in front of your body and raise them above your head. After you land on two feet, transfer your horizontal momentum to vertical as you jump again to the tossed ball. Pull both arms high and draw your hitting elbow back. Contact the ball with an open palm directly behind the center of the ball but slightly higher than you would on a standing serve. Drive your hand through the ball, keeping your palm square to the target zone. Land on the ground on both feet and proceed to your defensive position.

Figure 1.3 **JUMP FLOAT SERVE**

Preparation

1. Stand three or four steps behind the end line close to defensive assignment.
2. Square feet, hips, and shoulders to target.
3. Put weight on dominant foot.
4. Hold ball in nondominant hand.
5. Take a step and toss the ball forward and in front of hitting shoulder.

Serve

1. Jump forward off one foot.
2. Land on both feet as you pull both arms in front of body and raise them above head.
3. Jump again to tossed ball.
4. Pull both arms high and draw hitting elbow back.
5. Contact the ball with open palm directly behind center of ball.

Follow-Through

1. Drive hand through ball.
2. Keep palm square to target zone.
3. Land on floor on both feet.
4. Move to defensive position.

MISSTEP

Player uses a high toss for the jump float serve.

CORRECTION

The jump float toss should be higher than the contact point in order to reduce the chance for error. The higher the toss, the more variability in the contact that follows. You want the serve to be as consistent as possible.

Jump Spin Serve

The harder and higher a server strikes the ball on a topspin serve, the more effective it will be. The higher contact point allows the trajectory of the serve to be flatter, thus getting to the opponent's court faster. The harder the ball is struck, the steeper the ball will dive on the tail end of its path to the opponent's court. The challenge with this serve is the risk versus reward.

Olympic male and female volleyball players are capable of jump spin serves at speeds of 55 to 70 mph (88-113 km/h)! When contacting the ball with that kind of force, hand placement on the ball must be perfect. Even the slightest mistake will serve the ball wildly out of bounds. While the jump spin serve may look impressive, it is seldom effective except at elite levels.

For the jump spin serve (figure 1.4), position yourself three or four steps behind the end line close to your defensive assignment. Square your feet, hips, and shoulders to the zone in the opponent's court to which you are aiming. Put your weight on the same foot as your dominant arm and the ball in your non-dominant hand. Take a step and toss the ball forward and in front of the hitting shoulder. Jump forward off one foot but land on two feet as you pull both arms in front of your body and raise them above your head. Throw your attacking arm to the ball so that it is maximally extended at contact. Keeping your wrist relaxed, let your hand go from a contact point on the lower position on the ball to a higher position on the ball. Follow through by letting your hitting arm fall to your hip as you land on two feet and proceed to your defensive position.

Figure 1.4 JUMP SPIN SERVE

Preparation

1. Stand three or four steps behind the end line close to defensive assignment.
2. Square feet, hips, and shoulders to target.
3. Put weight on dominant foot.
4. Hold ball in nondominant hand.
5. Step and toss ball forward and in front of hitting shoulder.

Serve

1. Jump forward off one foot.
2. Land on two feet as you pull both arms in front of body and raise them above your head, jumping to the ball off two feet.
3. Throw attacking arm to the ball so that it is maximally extended at contact.
4. Keep wrist relaxed.
5. Let hand go from a lower position on the ball to a higher position on the ball.

Follow-Through

1. Let hitting arm fall to hip.
2. Land on two feet.
3. Move to defensive position.

MISSTEP

Player swings aggressively at the ball even if the ball is imperfectly tossed.

CORRECTION

Know how to adjust the speed of your arm swing when you toss the ball too far forward or misalign the toss with your body. Just because you have a bad toss doesn't entitle you to an error. Make the adjustment and keep the ball in play even if it is a little less aggressive.

Serving Variations

The float and spin serves are the standard serves in today's game, but there are many variations. Some jump servers take off from one leg, use a four-step approach to the ball, or use a very high toss to add speed and power to the serve. Some contact the ball more on the side when attempting a spin serve so that the ball veers to one side of the court or the other. A popular serve in outdoor volleyball is the sky ball, an underhanded serve that follows a high trajectory and causes the passers to look into the sun to track it.

SERVING TACTICS

Serving to different locations on the court can challenge your opponent and put your defense at an advantage. For beginning players, specific locations may also be easier to hit, leading to more consistent serves. Each player must weigh the risk–reward trade-off when choosing where to serve.

It is also advantageous to keep the trajectory of the serve as flat as possible. A higher or more arched trajectory gives the passer more time to get to the ball and get on balance. When the serve is flat, it reduces the time and can catch the opponent off-balance.

Because it is also more difficult for passers to track a ball coming at them (versus traveling across their visual field), a ball served directly at the opponent's shoulders can be challenging to pass. If you see that the passers are closer to the 10-foot (3 m) line than the end line when they are waiting for the serve, serve a fast, flat, and deep ball at their shoulders and force them to move backward to pass.

Serving Accuracy

Getting your serve in bounds is important, but it is also valuable to serve to specific locations on the court. Serving to specific zones can put your team in a position to score by serving to a particularly poor passer, making a strong hitter think about passing before attacking, or by simply putting people in the way of approaching hitters.

Serving zones are identified in the same way as serving order. Zone 1 is in the opponent's right-back position, zone 6 is in the middle-back position, and zone 5 is in the left-back position (figure 1.5). A coach or teammate might signal a server to serve to a particular zone number by showing the corresponding number of fingers. Zone 6 is typically signaled with a fist.

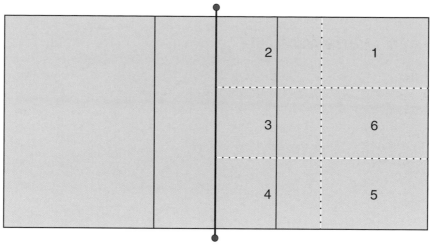

Figure 1.5 Serving zones.

Serving Short

Typically, teams will serve short if they have pulled a front-row player back into a serve-receive pattern, have exposed an open area of the court, or want to put a player passing the serve in the way of a quick hitter's approach pattern. To serve short, use a float serve and a lighter contact to give the ball enough of an arc to get over the net but not enough power to go deep in the court.

Risk vs. Reward

You don't want to serve so softly that the opponent is able to easily pass the ball and run their offense, but you don't want to serve so aggressively that you can't control the ball and keep it in play. Here are situations that would lead to being more conservative:

- Your teammates have missed a lot of serves.
- The rally preceding your serve could be a momentum starter.
- Your team is just coming out of a time-out.
- The other team is struggling (they probably won't win the point anyway, so don't miss your serve and make it easy on them).

When your opponents are likely to win the rally because of a very good hitter in the front row, it is better to be more aggressive than cautious. They will probably win the rally anyway, so you might as well hope for an ace!

EVALUATING THE SERVE

A service ace is when a serve directly results in a point for the serving team. An ace could happen if a served ball lands in the court untouched or if it is touched by the opponent but cannot be kept in play. It is also considered an ace when a receiving player illegally contacts the served ball (a block or lift, for instance) or when the receiving team is out of rotation. A ball that is passed poorly and that the setter mishandles is not considered an ace but still results in a point for the serving team.

A service error occurs when the served ball fails to cross the net, lands out of bounds, touches an antenna, or touches a player on the serving team before crossing the net. A service error also occurs when the server illegally contacts the ball (lift or double contact), tosses the ball twice, touches the end line before the ball leaves her hand, or is out of rotation.

Serving Drill 1   **Around the World**

Divide the court into six zones (figure 1.6). The goal of this drill is to accurately serve into each zone in successive order before missing a serve. You can do this drill by yourself or with a partner. Be sure to understand that the riskier side of the zone is near the out-of-bounds line. There is no penalty for serving in the court but out of the zone, but the penalty for serving out is starting over. The first player (or pair) to serve the ball to all six zones is the winner.

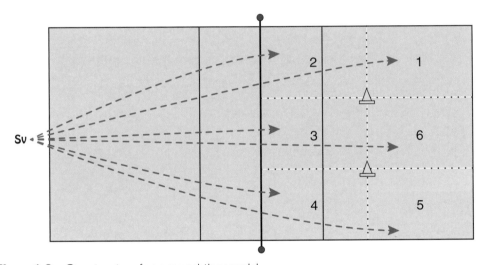

Figure 1.6   Court setup for around the world.

TO INCREASE DIFFICULTY

• Serve to each zone in order without serving out of bounds or in a nontargeted zone. If you serve to an area of the court you were not aiming at, start over.

TO DECREASE DIFFICULTY

• Allow serves to go out or to an alternative zone, but keep track of how many serves it takes to accurately serve one ball into each of the six zones.

Success Check

- Stand square to the target.
- Drive your hand through the center of the ball.
- Hold your palm to the target.

Score Your Success

Serve to all six zones in less than 2 minutes = 10 points

Serve to all six zones in 2 to 4 minutes = 5 points

Serve to all six zones in more than 4 minutes = 1 point

Your score ___

Serving Drill 2   Zones 1 Through 5

The goal of this drill is to serve accurately under pressure. Because most teams put their best passer in zone 6, eliminate that zone from being an in serve (use cones or a bed sheet to identify the area). Start with a goal of serving 15 balls in without hitting zone 6. For every ball served to zone 6 or out of bounds, add one to the goal. Servers serve one at a time to add gamelike pressure.

TO INCREASE DIFFICULTY

- Make zones 1 and 5 smaller by moving the cones closer to the sidelines.
- Add two serves to the goal for every ball served out of the target zone.

TO DECREASE DIFFICULTY

- Make zones 1 and 5 larger.
- Add a bonus point for serving multiple successful shots in a row.

Success Check

- Stand square to the target area.
- Take your time.
- Control your contact.

Score Your Success

Finish in 15 to 20 serves = 10 points

Finish in 21 to 25 serves = 5 points

Finish in 26 serves or more = 1 point

Your score ___

Serving Drill 3   **Short and Deep**

Use cones to designate an area of the court that is 4 feet (1.2 m) from the end line to 10 feet (3 m) from the end line the entire width of the court (figure 1.7). Count how many times you can serve accurately by alternating between the two spaces (short and deep). If you serve into the middle, remember your high score and start over.

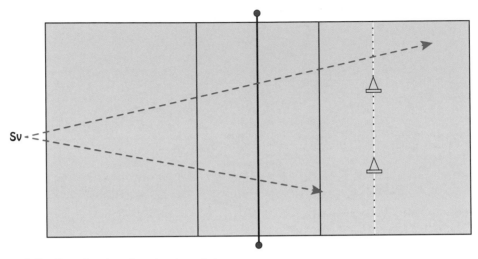

Figure 1.7   Court setup for short and deep.

TO INCREASE DIFFICULTY
- Make the target areas smaller.
- Move the short serving area closer to the net.
- Limit yourself to alternating between specific short and deep zones (1 and 4, for instance).

TO DECREASE DIFFICULTY
- Increase the size of the target areas.
- Move the short serving area deeper in the court.
- Eliminate the middle area between the short and deep and work on alternating across the line.
- Keep track of how many accurate serves you can accomplish during a time frame instead of assessing successive serves.

Success Check

- Stand square to the target area.
- Manipulate your arm swing speed for short and deep serves.
- Adjust your hand contact on the ball: lower for short serves and higher for deep serves.

7 or more successive serves alternating to short and deep locations = 10 points

4 to 6 successive serves alternating to short and deep locations = 5 points

3 or fewer successive serves alternating to short and deep locations = 1 point

Your score ___

Serving Drill 4 Elastic Serving

Take a length of elastic and tie it from one antenna to the other and slide it to the top. Practice serving under the elastic to keep the trajectory of your serve low. Serve six balls in a row below the elastic before serving two over the elastic or one out of bounds.

TO INCREASE DIFFICULTY

- Make your goal higher.
- Lower the height of the elastic.
- Add a target zone in the deep court.

TO DECREASE DIFFICULTY

- Allow yourself one more error over the elastic before you have to start over.
- Increase the height of the elastic.

Success Check

- Contact is higher on the ball to ensure a flat trajectory.
- Your palm faces the target after contact.

Score Your Success

6 or more serves = 10 points

3 to 5 serves = 5 points

Fewer than 3 serves = 1 point

Your score ___

SUCCESS SUMMARY

Being able to serve effectively is an important start to every player's skill set. If getting the serve over the net is challenging, use an underhand serve in competition but continue to practice the overhand serve by moving closer to the net to gain confidence and hone your technique. As your serving skill grows, practice serving consistently to different locations on the court. The ability to serve to any zone without fear of missing the serve will aid your team's ability to put your opponent on the defensive. Only after being able to consistently serve in the court and then accurately to each zone of the court, should you work on increasing the speed of your serve.

As you are competing, evaluate the effectiveness of your serve by judging the quality of the pass by your opponent. If your opponent makes a good pass, try serving to a different player or serving in a different way. If your opponent makes a bad pass, stay on that player consistently. The last thing you want to do is take the pressure off a struggling passer by missing your serve.

Use the four drills in this step to assess whether you are ready to progress to the next step. Out of the 40 points available, you should be able to demonstrate the accuracy and consistency required to achieve at least 70 percent (or 28 points). If you struggle to achieve this kind of consistency, find time to practice or use strategies to decrease difficulty. Remember that each step in the process builds on the last, and serving is the foundation for every rally. You want to be confident in this skill before taking the next step.

Serving Drills

1.	Around the world	___out of 10
2.	Zones 1 through 5	___out of 10
3.	Short and deep	___out of 10
4.	Elastic serving	___out of 10
	Total	**___out of 40**

Passing

For the receiving team, the pass is their first opportunity to set up their offensive system and put them in a position to score a point. A good pass will allow the setter to distribute the ball to multiple hitters and prevent blockers from ganging up on an individual hitter. A poor pass makes it difficult to set with accuracy and limits the hitters who are available to attack. This makes it easy for the defense to get into positions that increase their chances of winning the rally.

EVALUATING PASSING

Before understanding how to pass, it is important to understand what makes a pass perfect. While different teams may have different passing tactics, most teams define a perfect pass as one that is

- passed to the area of the net 3 feet, 4 inches to 6 feet, 7 inches (1-2 m) to the right of the middle of the net, making it easy for the setter to set all three hitters in the front row;

- passed high enough that the setter can stand tall to deliver the set, but not so high that it challenges the setter's ability to handle the ball; and

- passed within 6 feet, 7 inches (2 m) of the net, allowing for a quick middle attack.

Passes are evaluated on a 4-point scale (3, 2, 1, and 0). A 3-point pass is a perfect pass that allows the setter to set to all three hitters with ease and is tight enough to the net to hold the opponent's middle blockers in the middle of the court. A 2-point pass is a good pass, but one that prevents one hitter from being set either because it is too low, too far forward or back, or too tight or off the net. A 1-point pass refers to a pass that causes the setter to run after the ball and make a difficult set to the safest hitter or a pass that requires a nonsetter to set the ball. A 0-point pass refers to a pass that cannot be set either because no one can get to the ball to make a second contact or because it is passed directly over the net to the serving team. This evaluation system will be used in a variety of volleyball drills and is a common way for coaches to describe a team's passing efficiency.

PASSING TECHNIQUES

Every perfect pass begins with preparation that puts your body in a position to react quickly and move to the ball. As with many sport skills, the simplest movements are the most repeatable. If you want to be a consistent passer, it is important that your technique be simple and well trained.

When preparing to receive the ball, face the source of the ball (e.g., the server). Your feet arc shoulder-width apart, with the right foot slightly in front of the left and your weight forward and on the balls of your feet. Bend your knees so that they are over the tops of your toes. Flex slightly at the waist so that the shoulders are forward and over the tops of your knees. Your elbows are bent with the palms out (figure 2.1).

Figure 2.1 PASSING PREPARATION POSTURE

The following outlines the proper posture for receiving the ball:

1. Facing source of ball.
2. Feet shoulder-width apart, right foot slightly in front of left.
3. Weight on balls of feet.
4. Knees bent.
5. Shoulders over knees.
6. Elbows bent and palms out.

One of the most common problems novice volleyball players have is expecting the ball to come to them instead of moving to the ball. Footwork patterns that keep you square to the server and balanced will ensure more consistent passing results. Because it is rare that a served ball will land on the court more than a couple steps from a player, our focus will be on perfecting a footwork pattern that is simple and easy to use. The step-hop (figure 2.2) keeps the passer squared to the server and can be used to pursue a ball in any direction.

For the step-hop, start in ready position. Take a step in the direction of the ball's path with the foot closest to where the ball will land. Hop so that you land on both feet with your right foot slightly in front of the left. Practice with your first step going forward, right, left, and back while never crossing your feet over.

Figure 2.2 **STEP-HOP**

Step

1. Get in ready position.
2. Step in the direction of the ball's path with the foot closest to where the ball will land.

Hop

1. Hop and land on both feet.
2. Right foot is slightly in front of left.
3. Do not cross feet over.

The goal of your footwork should be to get your body behind the path of the ball and in the desired ready position to begin the passing skill.

Forearm Linear Passing

When you have successfully used your footwork to get your body behind the ball's path and your contact point with the ball is below your neck, you will perform the most controlled and consistent passing technique: forearm linear passing (figure 2.3). By lining up your arms, you will present to the ball a flat platform from which it can rebound toward your target. This technique is referred to as linear because your contact is happening with your body behind the platform, providing maximum strength and stability and ensuring that the ball rebounds forward toward the net. Passing to target with consistency is difficult and requires finesse more than strength.

Here are the keys to passing when your body is behind the path of the ball and your contact point is low. First call the ball by saying "mine" or "I" to let all of your teammates know that you intend to play the ball. Extend your arms out to the ball's path and lock your elbows. Place the backs of the fingers on your right hand on top of the fronts of your fingers on your left hand and align your thumbs so that they are parallel. Turn your thumbs to the ground so that your elbows come together and present a flat platform with your forearms. As the ball contacts the largest area of your forearms, transfer your weight from your back foot to your front foot while limiting the swing of your platform at the shoulder. Hold your shoulders strong to create a strong, stable platform and minimize your arm swing. After making contact with the ball, hold your contact position for one second to check for proper execution of the skill.

Figure 2.3 **FOREARM LINEAR PASS**

Preparation

1. Call for the ball.
2. Extend arms into ball's path.
3. Lock elbows.
4. Align fingers and thumbs.
5. Turn thumbs to ground.

Contact

1. Contact ball on largest area of forearms.
2. Transfer weight from back foot to front foot.
3. Limit the swing of the platform at the shoulder.

Follow-Through

1. Hold contact position for one second.
2. Return to ready position.

In any finesse skill, the least amount of movement generally results in greater consistency. For this reason, you will find success by limiting the swinging of the platform, avoiding crossover footwork patterns, and by holding your position immediately after making contact with the ball.

MISSTEP

You pass the ball over the net on the first contact.

CORRECTION

Usually, this is the result of contacting too far behind the ball and not enough under it. Practice contacting the ball and directing it where you want it to go.

MISSTEP

Player passes the ball too far off the net.

CORRECTION

Usually this is the result of contacting too much under the ball and not enough behind it. Experiment with where you contact the ball. By sticking your pass and watching where it goes, you give yourself feedback so you can improve your technique.

Forearm Nonlinear Passing

On occasion, it will be difficult to get your body all the way behind a ball and you may need to reach your platform to the right or left outside of your shoulders. While this technique is not as consistent as linear passing, it can still result in an accurate pass if you dip the forward shoulder to get the forearms behind the ball's path. With a slight shrug of the shoulders and a weight transfer in your feet, you will be able to direct the ball toward the net.

To execute the forearm nonlinear pass (figure 2.4), begin by moving your body as close to the ball as possible. Turn your torso in the direction of the ball and dip the shoulder opposite the ball. Extend your elbows and bring your hands together as you did for the forearm linear pass. Move your platform behind the path of the ball. Keep your shoulders strong and maximize the surface area for the contact. Minimize your swing as you redirect the ball to the target area. After contact, hold your contact position for one second, keeping your shoulders strong and dipped in the direction of the target. Then return to ready position to prepare for your next play.

Figure 2.4 FOREARM NONLINEAR PASS

Preparation

1. Get close to the ball.
2. Turn torso in ball's direction.
3. Dip shoulder opposite ball.
4. Extend elbows.
5. Bring hands together.

Contact

1. Move platform behind ball.
2. Keep shoulders strong.
3. Maximize surface area at contact.
4. Minimize swing.
5. Redirect ball to target.

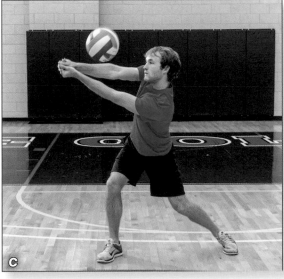

Follow-Through

1. Hold contact position for one second.
2. Keep shoulders strong and dipped toward target.
3. Return to ready position.

Overhead Passing

For serves deep in the court, you should step-hop backward (while facing the server) and pass the ball with your platform. In fact, many divisions of the game are establishing rules to prevent passing the serve with your hands. Some divisions (college volleyball for instance) still allow overhead passing (figure 2.5) and it can be a useful technique to cover more area of the court. A more detailed description of the technique can be found in step 3 on setting (the two skills are foundationally the same), but here are the steps in the process.

Move your arms from the ready position at your hips to your forehead with bent elbows. Your hands are wide open with the palms facing each other. Your thumbs are pointed back at your eyes. Bend the knees. Let the ball enter your hands and contact it with every fingertip and thumb. At contact with the ball, simultaneously extend the arms and legs while stepping forward. Extend the thumbs through the ball until your palms face the target. Hold the extension while balanced on your front foot.

MISSTEP

You get too far under the ball so that it contacts your hands but continues in its path to the end line.

CORRECTION

Make sure you get your hands behind the ball's path to ensure it travels forward where your teammates can keep it off the floor.

Figure 2.5 **OVERHEAD PASS**

Preparation

1. Get in ready position with arms at hips.
2. Lift arms to forehead, elbows bent.
3. Hands are wide open, palms facing each other.
4. Thumbs point back at eyes.

Contact

1. Bend knees.
2. Contact ball on fingertips and thumbs.
3. Extend arms and legs while stepping forward.

Follow-Through

1. Extend thumbs through ball.
2. Face palms toward target.
3. Hold extension while balanced on front foot.
4. Step through with back foot.
5. Return to ready position.

Most rule books allow the ball to be double contacted for the team's first play at the ball, so the execution of the overhead pass does not need to be completely clean. However, a player cannot catch or throw the ball; that would result in a point for the opponent.

Emergency Techniques

In an era in which players are able to jump serve at 70 miles per hour (113 km/h), sometimes a passer may need to dive for a ball or use an emergency technique. The most important goals when making emergency moves to the ball are to keep the ball on your side of the net and give your teammate a chance to continue the rally. Be sure to make your contact far enough under the ball that it rebounds high (figure 2.6). The increased height of the pass will give your teammates time to get to the ball even if it is heading toward the bleachers. You should also try to get your contact point on the outside of the ball to direct it back to the middle of the court where your teammates are ready. When an opponent serves tough, the margin of error on your pass is high. Instead of trying to pass perfectly, pass with height and to the middle of the court to give your teammates the opportunity to set a hitter.

Figure 2.6 **EXECUTING THE EMERGENCY PASS**

Preparation

1. Move quickly to the ball.
2. Extend platform to the ball.
3. Dip shoulder toward target.

Contact

1. Stiffen shoulders for contact.
2. Move platform behind the ball's path.
3. Direct extended arms forward and up to play the ball high.

Follow-Through

1. Hold arms extended for one second.
2. Return to ready position.

Passing Drill 1
Partner Distance Passing

With a partner, pass the ball back and forth, standing on the same side of the court, using the following criteria:

- Short passing: Stand 5 feet (1.5 m) away from each other. Focus on making solid platform contact and extending the arms straight to the ball.
- Medium passing: Stand 12 feet (3.6 m) away from each other. Add a focus on weight transfer from left leg to right leg.
- Long passing: Stand 20 feet (6.1 m) away from each other. Add a focus on leg extension during the weight transfer.

TO INCREASE DIFFICULTY

- Reduce the allowable height of the passes to 6 feet (1.8 m).
- Move from distance to distance without letting the ball drop.
- Allow only linear passes.

TO DECREASE DIFFICULTY

- Catch the ball when getting out of control and begin again.
- Pass the ball higher to give your partner more time to get to the ball.

Success Check

- Make contact on a solid platform.
- Extend the arms straight to the ball.
- Transfer the weight from the left leg to the right leg.
- Extend the legs during the weight transfer.

Score Your Success

20 or more passes in a row at each distance = 10 points

10 to 19 passes in a row at each distance = 5 points

9 or fewer passes in a row at each distance = 1 point

Your score ___

Passing Drill 2
Pass to Self and Nonlinear Pass to Partner

Position your platform under the ball so that you pass straight up in the air and move sideways so that the ball is off your midline. Drop your shoulder and contact around the ball to pass nonlinearly to your partner who is standing 20 feet (6.1 m) away.

TO INCREASE DIFFICULTY

- Decrease the height of the pass to yourself.
- Have your partner move farther away.

TO DECREASE DIFFICULTY

- Pass higher to yourself.
- Have your partner stand 10 feet (3 m) away.

Success Check

- Get your platform under and behind the ball.
- Drop your shoulder to your target.
- Limit your arm swing before and after contact.

Score Your Success

10 partner exchanges in a row = 10 points

5 to 9 partner exchanges in a row = 5 points

4 or fewer partner exchanges in a row = 1 point

Your score ___

Passing Drill 3
Pass and Move (Side to Side, Forward and Back)

Pass the ball to your partner. While the ball is in the air, step-hop to the right (figure 2.7). After your partner makes contact with the ball, step-hop back to the left so that you arrive to pass the ball from the same spot where you passed it before. Repeat but move in the opposite direction and continue to alternate. You should always pass the ball from the same location on the court.

Repeat the drill but use step-hop footwork to move forward and back. Again you should always pass the ball in the same position.

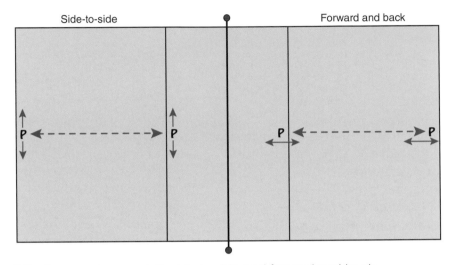

Figure 2.7 Pass-and-move drill: side to side and forward and back.

TO INCREASE DIFFICULTY

- Reduce pass height to increase speed of passing.
- Challenge yourself by extending your footwork between passes.

TO DECREASE DIFFICULTY

- Pass higher to give your partner more time to get to the ball.
- Stay close to the contact point of the ball by taking smaller steps.

Success Check

- Stay balanced during the pass and movement.
- Use step-hop footwork.
- Present your platform directly to the ball.
- Limit your arm swing.

PASSING LOCATION AND HEIGHT

The definition of a perfect pass varies depending on the characteristics of each team. A team with a tall setter and a quick offense might want to pass the ball 18 inches (45.7 cm) higher than the net and tight. A less advanced team might want to keep the ball off the net in order to give their setter more room to maneuver. Optimal passing location and height can be influenced by whether or not the setter is in the front or back row or how adept she is at attacking the second contact (referred to as a setter dump).

Typically, most teams pass the ball 3 feet, 4 inches to 6 feet, 7 inches (1-2 m) from the middle of the net. Passing the ball to this location allows a team to easily set all three hitters in the front row. Because setting forward is easier than setting backward and setting off the net is easier to attack than setting too tight to the net, consider the following challenges in pass locations:

- A ball passed left of center will be difficult to set backward to the right-side hitter and will prevent the setter from seeing the quick middle attacker coming in behind her.
- A ball passed too far to the right of center will require the setter to move backward and lose a forward weight transfer, allowing the ball to be pushed to the left antenna.
- A ball passed too far off the net will force the setter to set toward the net, a challenging skill to prevent the ball from drifting too tight to the block.
- A ball passed too tight to the net will risk the setter contacting the net and losing some of his strength in being able to extend linearly from the legs through the arms and hands.
- A ball passed too low will force the setter to use a forearm pass to distribute the ball, resulting in a slower and more predictable offense.

- A ball passed too high provides the defensive team ample time to prepare for the offense. High passes also require very strong setting hands to prevent a double contact because of the ball's acceleration as it descends.

Ideal passing location can be adapted to meet the needs of your team but it is imperative that everyone understands where that location is and when it changes. Communication between passers, setters, and hitters ensures that everyone is prepared for this important contact.

Passing Drill 4   **Butterfly**

The butterfly drill is a serving and passing drill in which you follow the ball that you just contacted. Six players (three on each side) are required for this full-court drill, but it can accommodate as many as 24. Players are located on both sides of the net, with a server at the serving line in zone 1, the target at the net, and the passer in zone 5. Both   sides serve the ball at the same time to the passer on the opposite side of the net (figure 2.8). The passers pass to the target, and the target catches the pass before it hits the floor. The target takes the ball and becomes the next server. The server follows the serve and becomes the next passer on the opposite side of the net, and the passer becomes the next target. The objective of this drill is to achieve 30 passes to target in 3 minutes.

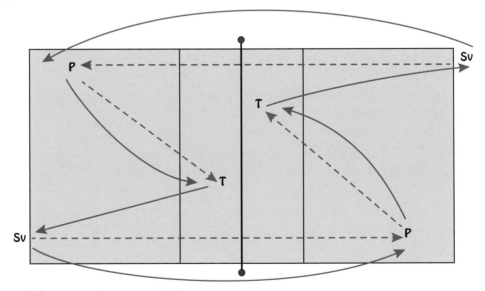

Figure 2.8   Butterfly passing drill.

TO INCREASE DIFFICULTY

- Require serves to be lower than the antenna.
- Require the target to catch the ball above her head.
- Subtract a pass for every serve that lands in the court untouched.
- Add a pass to the goal for any missed serve.

TO DECREASE DIFFICULTY

- Remove the time constraint.
- Count every pass regardless of quality.
- Do not assess a penalty for missed serves.

Success Check

- Get in ready position before serve.
- Use the step-hop footwork to achieve balance.
- Extend your platform directly behind the ball's path.
- Hold your contact position without swinging your arms.

Score Your Success

30 passes or more in 3 minutes = 10 points

15 to 29 passes in 3 minutes = 5 points

Fewer than 15 passes in 3 minutes = 1 point

Your score ___

Passing Drill 5   Four-Passer Weave With Scoring

The passing weave drill requires passers to stay focused and understand their passing responsibilities while practicing strong technique. Three passers divide the court into three lanes, with one passer waiting to come in, while servers on the other side of the net initiate the drill. If a passer in a lane next to a sideline passes the ball, he exits the drill, the passer in the middle moves over to replace him, and the new passer comes into the middle (figure 2.9). If the passer in the middle passes the ball, the side passers stay and the middle passer is replaced by the waiting player. Pass for three minutes. The drill becomes more challenging when the speed of serving increases.

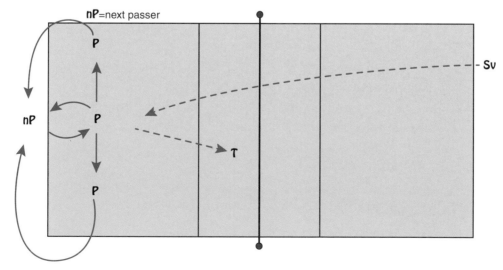

Figure 2.9   Four-passer weave with scoring.

(continued)

Passing Drill 5 *(continued)*

TO INCREASE DIFFICULTY

- Increase the speed at which balls are served.
- Decrease the time between serves.
- Serve successively to the same position.

TO DECREASE DIFFICULTY

- Serve balls that follow a loftier trajectory.
- Wait until everyone is in proper position before serving.

Success Check

- Communicate by calling the ball when you are going to take it.
- Use the step-hop footwork to achieve balance when making the pass.
- Extend your platform directly behind and under the path of the served ball.
- Hold your contact position for one second.

Score Your Success

30 passes or more to target in 3 minutes = 10 points

15 to 29 passes to target in 3 minutes = 5 points

Fewer than 15 passes to target in 3 minutes = 1 point

Your score ___

SERVE-RECEIVE SYSTEMS

When playing recreational volleyball, it may not be important to maximize your team's serve = receive efficiency, but when passing quality is one of the statistics most closely related to winning, competitive teams want to be as efficient as possible. Here are a few fundamental principles to consider when designing a serve-receive system for your team:

- Put your best passers where they can pass the most balls, usually the middle of the court or zone 6.
- Allow your passers to specialize by passing from areas on the court with which they are most familiar.
- Exploit your passers' strengths and hide their weaknesses.
- Position your setter as close to the passing target as possible.
- Position your hitters so that their approach patterns are clear and unobtrusive.

Not every player on the court has to pass. A team can move players to the net or hide them in a corner to give better passers more responsibility while maintaining rotational order. Some players have a talent for passing while others do not, and there is no reason to have a bad passer responsible for significant areas of the court. Remember, you cannot control to whom an opponent decides to serve. Most teams use a three-passer system to divide the court into three lanes.

A three-passer system provides a team the opportunity to put their best passers in positions to pass the most balls, reduces the amount of open court space without adding the challenge of more seams between players, and clearly defines each player's responsibilities on the court. Since the rules were changed allowing serves that contact the net to still be in play, many teams pull a front-row player to the middle of the court at the 10-foot (3 m) line to defend short serves.

A team might decide to pass with only two passers instead of three. A two-passer system will ensure that only the best passers are making the first contact, but it also makes more area of the court vulnerable to an ace.

A team may choose to put every player except the setter in the passing pattern. While this covers more area of the court, it also provides more opportunity for communication errors when a ball is served between two players.

Consider several factors when designing a serve-receive system for your team; all have positives and negatives. Be sure to think through the possibilities when choosing a system. Also be prepared with a backup plan if your system isn't working.

MISSTEP

Five players prepare to pass serve when three are much better than the other two.

CORRECTION

Specialization helps to increase efficiency and puts players in positions to maximize their contributions to the team's success.

Passing Drill 6   Ace and Replace

Consistency in passing can be determined by a strong average in passing, but you can have a strong average with high variance. Using our 4-point passing evaluation scale, I would rather have a player who makes 2-point passes every time than a passer who has an equal number of 1 and 3 passes. They both average the same score (2.0), but the decreased variance helps the setter and the hitters know what to expect.

In this drill, 2- and 3-point passes are rewarded with 1 point. A 1-point pass allows you to stay as a passer, but you don't get points. An ace means that the server and the passer who missed the serve switch positions. It helps to have a coach (or a designated judge) allocate points and direct the action, but players can also do the same. Play continues in the drill, with players repeating the skills they are executing or replacing others based on the scoring system. The first passer to 5 points wins. Remember that even though you might make a 3-point pass, you get only 1 point toward your total.

TO INCREASE DIFFICULTY

- Decrease the number of passers on the court.
- Reduce the acceptable range for a two- or three-point pass.

(continued)

Passing Drill 6 *(continued)*

TO DECREASE DIFFICULTY

- Increase the number of passers on the court.
- Award 2 points for a two-point pass and 3 points for a three-point pass.

Success Check

- Serve tough to earn the opportunity to pass.
- Direct your platform under the ball to ensure a pass high enough to earn points.
- Use your legs to direct the ball to the target.
- Hold your contact positon for one second after contact.

Score Your Success

Pass 10 or more two- or three-point passes in 5 minutes = 10 points

Pass 5 to 9 two- or three-point passes in 5 minutes = 5 points

Pass fewer than 5 two- or three-point passes in 5 minutes = 1 point

Your score ___

Passing Drill 7 **Rotational Scramble**

This drill helps players become comfortable with rotational order and the way serve-receive systems are set up. A team of six players stands on both sides of the net. One player on each team is the designated setter. The instructor calls out a zone number to which the setter needs to go, and all players maintain rotational order on the court. Then the instructor designates three passers. Players must align themselves in a legal serve-receive pattern for the rotation identified. The team that creates a legal pattern first gets 1 point and a new setter location is called out. Repeat until the setter has been placed in each of the six zones of the court. If the score is tied at 3 to 3, break the tie by identifying an alternative pattern to the last one called.

TO INCREASE DIFFICULTY

- Call out rotations that are farther than two rotations away from the current rotation (3, 6, 2, 5, and so on).
- Require that players move directly to their zone without rotating.
- Serve a ball and have the team play it out.

TO DECREASE DIFFICULTY

- Call out successive rotations that move players in rotational order (1, 2, 3, and so on).
- Allow players to rotate to their spots instead of going directly to the zone.

Success Check

- Know who is opposite you (three rotations away).
- Know who is on your left and right.

ORGANIZING THE OFFENSE

One aspect of volleyball that makes it unique in the world of sports is the concept of rotating positions. Mike Hebert, the coaching legend and former head coach at the University of Minnesota, poses the question, "What if baseball players had to rotate positions every inning, each taking their turn at pitching, catching, infield, and outfield?" There is specialization in volleyball, but the rotational aspect of the game creates challenges. Besides trying to put the best passing personnel in the serve-receive pattern, you also want to consider how to run an effective offense even when hitters are out of position. For instance, when the left-side hitter is in the right-front position in serve receive, she either needs to work on attacking at the right antenna or the whole front row needs to move to the left side of the court to maintain rotation, but you also need to put your hitter where she can be most successful. Of course, after the serve is contacted, players can run wherever they want to (within the front row), but it is often more advantageous to have them approach at other places on the net. It gives the defense a different look from what they are used to seeing and can catch them off guard.

Consider the benefit of getting your setter as close as possible to the target passing location over putting your hitters in advantageous approach patterns. If your setter is slow, then putting her closest to the passing target might lead to more effective sets and a better chance of winning the rally.

Try to line up your best attacker against the opponent's weakest blocker. Executing this strategy in serve receive will allow you to take advantage of the matchup without having to switch positions.

Use the approach pattern to get a hitter closer to her base position, her specialized spot in the front or back row. When the left side is on the right side of the court, have her hit a high set in the middle of the court (described as a 52 in step 7) so that if the ball is dug, she is closer to her base defensive position. A quick dig and first-tempo attack can quickly catch a team unprepared if consideration isn't given to how you will get your players to their base positions out of serve receive.

When pulling a hitter back into the serve-receive pattern, make sure she focuses on passing first. Many hitters who pass serve rush their pass to start their approach. If you don't get a good pass, you won't get a good set. Focus on sticking your pass and adding a little height to put your setter, and yourself, in better position to be successful.

MISSTEP

You focus on the third contact when the problem is with the first or second.

CORRECTION

Focus your attention in the order of contacts. Put your team in the best position possible to get a quality pass then think about how to get a great set. Finally, think about your hitters and how their approach patterns affect their success.

Passing Drill 8   2-Point Passing Activation

This is a scrimmage drill that rewards serving and passing. Two teams of six players stand on the court, with one team the designated serving team. The quality of the pass for every rally determines which team has the potential to score a point. If the passing team passes the serve with a 2- or 3-point pass, they have the opportunity to score 1 point if they win the rally. If they do not win the rally, no point is awarded. If the passing team passes a 1- or 0-point pass and they win the rally, the serving team scores 1 point. The team that wins the rally chooses whether they want to serve or pass the next point. Play to 5 points and scramble teams.

TO INCREASE DIFFICULTY

- Reduce the acceptable range of a two-point pass.
- Do not assess a penalty for service errors.
- Set an upper and lower boundary for the pass height.

TO DECREASE DIFFICULTY

- Penalize service errors to force the serving team to be more conservative.

Success Check

- Stay relaxed when you pass.
- Strive for consistently good over inconsistently perfect.
- Serve tough to put the passing team on the defensive.

Score Your Success

Your team wins = 10 points

The other team wins = 5 points

Your score ___

SUCCESS SUMMARY

The ability to accurately pass the serve is one of the skills most related to winning. Players who are able to perform this skill effectively employ efficient footwork to get to the ball balanced and squared. When they contact the ball, they do so with as little movement as possible, simply redirecting the ball toward the target area. Holding the follow-through position reduces the movement even more, but it also allows the passer to evaluate her contact and make slight adjustments that improve control. Even in emergency situations, proficient passers will use efficient footwork, balance, and simplicity to keep the ball alive on their side of the net.

As you become more adept at passing, you will learn which situations require forearm and overhead passing techniques. You will also learn which situations allow you to put the ball right on the setter's forehead and which ones you should try to keep high and off the net. Regardless of the situation, the more often you can help your team get in system, the more valuable you will be in helping establish your team's offensive potential.

Before moving on to the next step on setting, make sure you have sufficiently mastered the passing techniques in this step. If you have scored at least 60 points in the drills, you are ready to take the next step. If you scored fewer than 60 points, go through the techniques that are giving you trouble and practice the drills again. Or try some of the variations that decrease difficulty.

Passing Drills

1.	Partner distance passing	___out of 10
2.	Pass to self and nonlinear pass to partner	___out of 10
3.	Pass and move (side to side, forward and back)	___out of 20
4.	Butterfly	___out of 10
5.	Four-passer weave with scoring	___out of 10
6.	Ace and replace	___out of 10
7.	Rotational scramble	___out of 10
8.	2-Point passing activation	___out of 10
	Total	___**out of 90**

Setting

The most significant difference between playing volleyball at the recreational and competitive levels is the role of the setter. When playing for fun at a family reunion, the player who sets usually is whomever is closest to the pass, but when playing competitively, a designated setter can make all the difference in executing a cohesive game plan that leads to success. A good setter can make up for passing deficiencies and help hitters find success. Designated setters are referred to as the quarterback on the court because, similar to the quarterback in football, they make decisions about who gets the ball and the opportunity to score. While they may not receive a lot of attention from the media, they are involved in almost every rally and are typically the most athletic players on a team. We will discuss the techniques and tactics a setter employs in order to facilitate an effective offense and help his or her team win.

OPTIMAL SET LOCATION

A setter should be concerned with four factors:

1. Distance
2. Depth
3. Height
4. Speed

The distance of the set determines the options a hitter has to attack. Balls that are set to the target location provide the hitter with multiple options for attacking down the line, hitting crosscourt, or using an off-speed shot (e.g., tip). How far the ball is set off or on the net (depth) determines the angles a hitter can attack around a block. When the ball is set tight to the net, the hitter can contact closer to the top of the ball, thus allowing for sharper attacking angles. When the ball is set farther off the net, the hitter must attack deeper and flatter shots.

Because balls set tight to the net are much easier to block, it is recommended that setters keep the ball 2 to 5 feet (.6-1.5 m) off the net to prevent trapping a hitter into a well-established block. Set trajectory and speed work together to create a rhythm and timing with a hitter. The height and speed of the set should be slow enough that it allows hitters to make a strong approach to the ball and an adequate adjustment to a slightly imperfect set. The set should not be so high and slow, however, that it provides the defense ample time to prepare their block and diggers. Finding a balance between speed and efficiency is what most teams spend a bulk of their season trying to master.

BASIC SETTING TECHNIQUE

As with passing, footwork is important to setting effectively (figure 3.1). Arriving at the ball balanced allows the hands to make a smooth and consistent contact. Officials require players to set the ball with both hands working in perfect coordination. If the setter is not balanced and squared to the target, he is likely to be called for a double contact. The movement principles outlined here will prepare you to make a consistently strong second contact and facilitate both the effectiveness of your set as well as your ability to deceive the opponent.

As soon as the ball is served or you know that you won't have to make the first contact, sprint to the target location and wait for the ball to get to you. Keep your eyes and shoulders facing the court as you run to the ball. Take lots of short steps instead of long strides so that you are able to change directions quickly if you need to.

After you have put your body in a position to stand tall, bring both hands up to your forehead, elbows bent. Point your thumbs back toward your eyes and make your hands soft and ready to surround the ball as it comes down toward your forehead. Stagger your feet with your left foot behind the right and point your right foot at the left antenna, regardless of whether you are setting forward or back. As the ball enters your hands, make contact with all 10 fingers, extend the elbows, and press your thumbs forward until the ball redirects to your target.

Setting is a finesse skill similar to passing, and the same rule applies to gain consistency: the less movement, the better. Novice players tend to have a grandiose follow-through that includes pointing their hands out and flailing their arms. These large movements increase the likelihood of a double contact with the ball. Use a quick, simple movement.

Figure 3.1 **BASIC SET**

Preparation

1. Sprint to the target location using short steps and changing directions as needed.
2. Wait for ball.
3. Face eyes and shoulders toward the court.
4. Place right foot in front of left.
5. Point toe at left antenna.

Contact

1. Lift both hands to forehead, elbows bent.
2. Point thumbs back toward eyes.
3. Keep hands soft.
4. Surround ball as it comes down.
5. Make contact with all 10 fingers.
6. Extend elbows and press thumbs forward to redirect ball to target.
7. As you make contact, transfer weight from back foot to front foot.
8. Maintain balance.

Follow-Through

1. Face target with elbows extended.
2. Shift from ball-shaped hands on contact to flat hands.
3. Hold extension for a brief moment and focus.
4. Execute a quick, simple release.
5. Let hands drop to the sides.

MISSTEP

You watch your set.

CORRECTION

After you have completed the set, cover your hitter. Follow your set and at the hitter's contact, get into a low, defensive ready position with your hands out and your eyes on the block. Often, the setter is in the best position to cover a ball blocked by the opponent.

OVERHEAD PASSING

The setting technique can be used by nonsetters to pass the ball on the first, second, or third contact. When back setting or deceiving the opponent's blockers is not a priority, the ball can be taken lower on the forehead with the body angled forward to provide additional resistance to the ball (figure 3.2).

To execute the overhead pass, first move your body into position so the ball's path is directed at your forehead. Stagger your feet with your right foot slightly in front of your left foot and shift your weight to your left foot. Keep your feet, hips, and shoulders square to the direction of the ball. Bring your hands to your head with your thumbs pointed back at your forehead. To make contact, move your hands directly behind the path of the ball. Maximize the contact surface area between the ball and your fingertips. Extend your elbows as you extend your knees. Move your thumbs forward until your palms face the target. After contact, hold a balanced position with your weight on your right foot. Return to ready position to prepare for your next play.

The advantage of overhead passing is the ability to pass the ball quickly with a low trajectory. A pass off the forearms requires a trajectory arc that the overhead pass doesn't.

Some areas of the United States and competitive levels are more sensitive to double-contact violations in overhead setting technique. The best strategy is to use forearm passing on challenging balls and if you get called for a double contact, learn what the standard is and make the adjustment.

Figure 3.2 **OVERHEAD PASS**

Preparation

1. Move so ball's path is aimed at your forehead.
2. Stagger feet with weight on left foot, with right foot slightly in front.
3. Square feet, hips, and shoulders to ball.
4. Turn thumbs to ground.

Contact

1. Move forearms directly behind ball's path.
2. Maximize contact surface area between ball and forearms.
3. Extend elbows and knees.

Follow-Through

1. Hold balanced position with weight on right foot.
2. Return to ready position for next contact.

MISSTEP

You time your movement to the ball so that you get to the pass at the same time as you need to set the ball.

CORRECTION

Beat the ball to where it is going so that you can bend your knees, square to your target, and see what is happening on the other side of the net.

Setting Drill 1 **Partner Distance Setting**

This drill is similar to the partner distance passing drill in step 2. With a partner who is 5 feet (1.5 m) away from you, work on your setting hands by keeping them in position above your head and with elbows extended. Set to your partner for 20 repetitions. Move back 7 feet (2.1 m) until you are about 12 feet (3.6 m) from your partner and add the elbow flexion and extension. Set another 20 balls. Move until you are 20 feet (6.1 m) from your partner and add the leg extension to practice the complete technique.

TO INCREASE DIFFICULTY

- Reduce the allowable height of the sets to 6 feet (1.8 m).
- Increase the minimum allowable height of sets to 20 feet (6.1 m).
- Move from distance to distance without letting the ball drop.

TO DECREASE DIFFICULTY

- Catch the ball when it's getting out of control and begin again.
- Set the ball between 10 and 12 feet (3-3.6 m) high to give your partner time to get to the ball.

Success Check

- Keep your weight on your left foot.
- Keep thumbs back on contact.
- Keep hands flat to target on release.
- Finish balanced on the right foot.

Score Your Success

15 to 20 sets in a row at 20 feet (6.1 m) = 10 points

10 to 14 sets in a row at 20 feet = 5 points

9 or fewer sets in a row at 20 feet = 1 point

Your score ___

Setting Drill 2 **Four-Corners Setting**

Divide players into four lines, each beginning at the corners of the court (end line and 10-foot [3 m] line). The ball should travel counterclockwise so that you are squaring up to the person to your left and setting along the line that is on your right (figure 3.3). Follow your set to the next line and continue the drill. When you have mastered keeping one ball going, add another at the opposite corner of the court. Can you handle four balls?

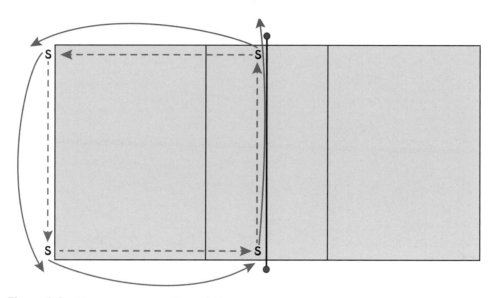

Figure 3.3 Four-corners setting drill.

TO INCREASE DIFFICULTY

- Add more balls to the drill.
- Coordinate the height of the simultaneously set balls.
- Allow players to forearm pass the ball to keep it off the floor.

TO DECREASE DIFFICULTY

- Catch the ball when it's getting out of control and begin again.
- Set the ball between 10 and 12 feet (3-3.6 m) high to give your teammates time to get to the ball.

Success Check

- Keep your weight on your left foot.
- Stay square to the target.
- Keep thumbs back on contact.
- Keep hands flat to target on release.
- Finish balanced on right foot.

Score Your Success

20 sets or more without a ball dropping = 10 points

10 to 19 successive sets = 5 points

9 or fewer successive sets = 1 point

Your score ___

Setting Drill 3 **Butterfly Drill With Setter**

Perform the same butterfly drill used in step 2, but add a setter where there was a target (figure 3.4). Six players, three on each side, prepare for the drill. The server is at the serving line in zone 1, the setter is at the net, and the passer is in zone 5. Both sides serve the ball at the same time to the passer on the opposite side of the net. The passers pass to the setters, who set the ball to the target after receiving the pass. The target moves to either the left- or right-side attacking position. In the butterfly drill you always follow your ball, so the setter follows the ball and becomes the target, who then moves to the serving location. The objective of the drill is to achieve 30 sets to the target.

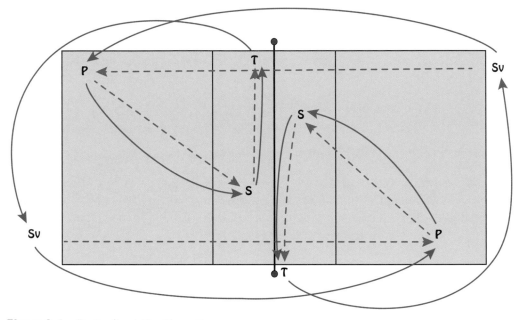

Figure 3.4 Butterfly drill with setter.

TO INCREASE DIFFICULTY

- Speed up the drill with serves made faster.
- Make the range of acceptable sets smaller.
- Have the setter back set to the right antenna.

TO DECREASE DIFFICULTY

- Slow the drill by making sure everyone is in position before the serve.
- Provide a larger target area for the setter.

Success Check

- Square up to the left antenna on every set.
- Balance on the front foot.
- Follow your set to get into coverage position.

SETTING TACTICS

Being able to accurately set to every hitter on the court is a function of both the setter's ability and the quality of the pass. From a perfect pass, the setter should be able to accurately set all hitters in the front or back rows. This section will help you distribute the offense to all available hitters.

Setting to the Left Antenna

The most common set in practically any volleyball game is to the left antenna (figure 3.5). In general, it is set forward where the setter has broad vision of the hitter and the hitter has plenty of time to adjust her approach to the ball in order to attack it with maximum power.

Figure 3.5 Setting the ball to the left antenna.

When setting forward to the left antenna, keep your contact point above your forehead. To give the ball a higher trajectory, contact under the ball and extend upward. To give the ball a flatter trajectory, contact behind the ball and extend forward. A higher trajectory gives the hitter more time, but it also gives the defense time to set a block and get into defensive position. A set with a flatter trajectory gets to the pin faster and can sometimes beat the block, giving the hitter an advantage before the block is well established. Unfortunately, a faster set also requires great coordination between the hitter and setter and can make imperfect sets difficult to attack.

Setting to the Right Antenna

To back set to the right antenna (figure 3.6), start by squaring to the left antenna. By consistently squaring to the left antenna, you will not give away to your opponent your setting intention. Bring your hands up to the same location on your forehead as you would to set forward, but put your body in a position to contact under the ball. Transfer weight forward to the left antenna and extend your elbows up and back. If you step through the ball, the ball will leave the hands when they are at the back of the head. When the pass takes you off the net, continue to square to the left antenna and, after contacting the ball, set over your right shoulder to direct the ball to the right side of the net.

Figure 3.6   Setting the ball to the right antenna.

Setting Middle

As with back setting, it is important that your preparation for setting the middle looks the same as any other set. The difference between setting the middle (figure 3.7) and other locations is in the contact point on the ball and the speed of the leg and elbow extension. Because you don't need to push the ball as far, your contact should be under the ball, and full extension of the legs and elbows is not necessary. The challenge in setting the middle is tempo. Most middle attacks are quicker sets, peaking lower than the height of the antenna. The speed of your release of the ball in your hands will determine the speed of the set.

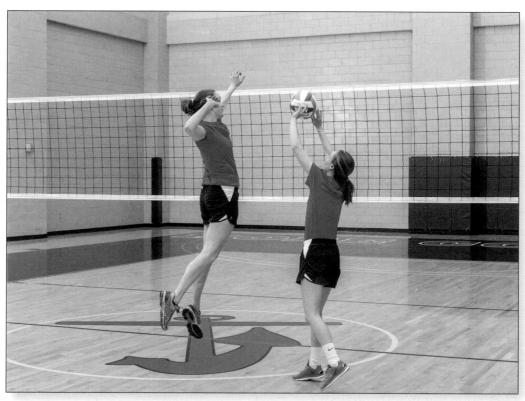

Figure 3.7   Setting the middle.

Setting Back Row

The back-row attack has become a popular offensive option over the years. When the pass is good, the back-row attack offers one more hitter for whom the defense needs to prepare; when the pass is bad, the back-row attack provides an option that is easier to set and more difficult to block. Because the back-row attacker is required to jump from behind the 10-foot (3 m) line, the set should lead the hitter across the 10-foot line, allowing the hitter to jump and land in the front court (figure 3.8). By remaining squared to the left antenna, you will have to set over your left shoulder to properly locate the ball 8 to 9 feet (2.4-2.7 m) off the net.

Figure 3.8 Setting to the back

Nonsetter Setting

A team's designated setter should try to make the second contact every time the ball is on her side of the net. On occasion, the setter will not be able to make that contact, either because of the quality of the pass or because she made the first contact. When a nonsetter must make the second contact, the safest set is usually the best one. Using a deep knee bend, the nonsetter should move directly under the ball, square up to the crosscourt antenna, and set at a high trajectory that is contacted 5 feet (1.5 m) off the net and 5 feet in from the sideline (figure 3.9). This set allows for maximal margin of error as well as ensuring the hitter has enough time and space to make a full attack.

Figure 3.9 Nonsetter setting.

Jump Setting

After you have mastered setting from the ground, try jump setting the ball (figure 3.10). Your footwork to the pass will be similar to setting from the ground, but instead of weight transferring onto your front foot, jump off both feet so that you meet the ball in the air. The jumping motion will provide the momentum needed to set the ball all the way to the antenna. Jump setting allows the setter to contact the ball higher, making the offense faster and allowing the passers to direct the ball higher, flatter, and quicker to the target area.

Figure 3.10 The jump set.

Excellent setters are able to identify many things in their visual field that lead to effective setting. While keeping their focal vision on the passed ball, setters can use their peripheral vision to see the speed of approaching hitters, the attacking arm of a quick hitter, whether or not the middle blocker is releasing early to a specific hitter, or whether a blocker is lining up in such a way as to take away a specific attack. If you see a hitter is late in starting her approach, you can add height to the set so she has enough time to go through her full approach. If you see the opponent's middle blocker releasing to the left-side hitter before you have set the ball, you can set backward to the right-side hitter, who will have a solo block. Once you are comfortable with knowing what the ball is doing, attend to factors in your peripheral vision to identify competitive opportunities.

Setting Tactics Drill 1   **Location Setting**

From the backcourt, a coach tosses a ball to a player at the setting position just right of center. The setter sets the ball to a target located at any of the three locations discussed in this step (left front, middle, or right front; figure 3.11). After the set has been made, the setter gets into coverage position. Special consideration should be given to erring on the side of setting inside and off the net. The setter returns to base position and another ball is tossed until she has set 20 balls.

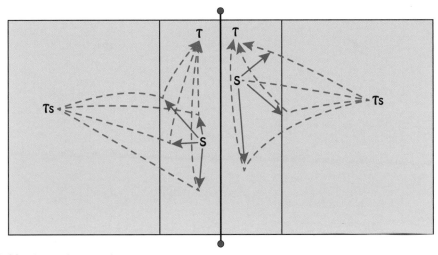

Figure 3.11   Location setting.

TO INCREASE DIFFICULTY

- Require that the ball follow a specific arc in addition to landing in the target area by placing an antenna on the net where the apex of the ball's path should be.
- Require the setter to run from the back row to the setter position every time.
- Require the setter to come from a blocking position in the right front.
- Toss the ball to the setter imperfectly (too far forward, off the net, backward, or tight).
- Require a certain number (five, for instance) of perfect consecutive sets.

TO DECREASE DIFFICULTY

- Increase the size of the target area.
- Make every toss to the setter position.

Success Check

- Open yourself to the pass.
- Keep thumbs back on contact.
- Keep hands flat to target on release.
- Finish balanced on right foot and squared to left antenna.

Score Your Success

16 or more out of 20 sets to target = 10 points

10 to 15 out of 20 sets to target = 5 points

9 or fewer out of 20 sets to target = 1 point

Your score ___

Setting Tactics Drill 2   **Setting Against the Flow**

Establish a target at both the right and left antennae (figure 3.12). The ball is tossed to a setter who is coming from the back row. The toss either leads the setter forward or pushes him back. The setter should set in the direction opposite from where the pass is bringing him. The setter should apply proper technique and balance on the front foot regardless of which direction he sets. The setter returns to base positon and repeats the drill for 10 attempts.

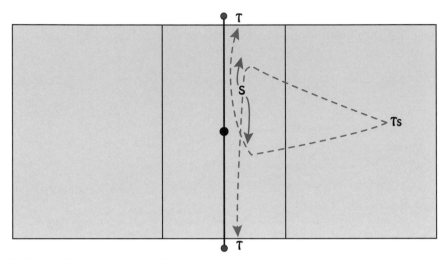

Figure 3.12   Setting against the flow.

TO INCREASE DIFFICULTY

- Make the target smaller.
- Instead of a toss, an attacker hits the ball to the setter.

TO DECREASE DIFFICULTY

- The tosser tells the setter where the ball is going.
- The tosser tosses the ball high to give the setter more time.

Success Check

- Balance on your front foot.
- Practice proper setting technique.

Score Your Success

Earn 1 point for each successful set (10 attempts).

Your score ____

Setting Tactics Drill 3   **Setting Against the Middle**

Multiple minigames happen within the course of a rally. One of those games is between the setter and the opposing middle blocker. In this drill, the objective is for the setter to see an early releasing middle and set away from where the middle is going. A player tosses a ball to a setter at the passing target location, with a middle blocker on the opposite side of the net. Just before the ball gets to the setter's hands, the middle moves left or right up to the blocker. The setter, while focusing on the ball and seeing the block in his peripheral vision, should set in the direction opposite from the way the blocker moves. The drill can also be run for the blocker; have the blocker try to read the setter and move in the direction the setter is going to set.

TO INCREASE DIFFICULTY

- The middle leaves later (or closer to when the setting contact is made).
- The coach tosses the ball off the net so that it is more difficult for the setter to see the middle.
- The middle cheats in the easier direction to set the ball, forcing the setter into the more difficult set.

TO DECREASE DIFFICULTY

- The instructor tosses every ball directly to the setter.
- The middle leaves well before the ball arrives at the setter.
- The middle leaves in the direction of the harder set, forcing the setter into the easier set.

Success Check

- Use peripheral vision to see the middle leave early.
- Square to the left antenna on every ball.
- Keep a neutral contact point.

Score Your Success

Set in the correct direction 8 times or more = 10 points

Set in the correct direction 5 to 7 times = 5 points

Set in the correct direction fewer than 5 times = 1 point

Your score ____

SUCCESS SUMMARY

Setting your team requires you to have strong technical skill and tactical awareness. Develop your ability to square to the left antenna. Keep your thumbs back until you press your hands and elbows forward. Finish the set with flat hands and balanced on your right foot. Follow these keys and your consistency and accuracy will improve. Optimally, your hitter's effectiveness will improve as well, and you will be able to accurately get the ball to all three hitters from multiple locations on the court.

As you consider the speed with which you are going to set your hitters, try to strike a balance between setting fast enough to keep your opponent off balance and giving your hitter enough time to generate the power necessary to take a big swing. Taking all of these factors into consideration will help you facilitate the success of your team's offense.

A good set leads to a great attack. The setter shoulders an awesome responsibility for giving her attacker the best set to hit. Practice the techniques and drills in this step. Once you have scored at least 40 points, you are ready to move to the next step on attacking. If you have trouble scoring at least 40 points, go through the drills again, focusing on the techniques that are challenging for you. Try some of the variations to decrease difficulty to lift your scores and your confidence.

Setting Drills

1. Partner distance setting   ___out of 10
2. Four-corners setting   ___out of 10
3. Butterfly drill with setter   ___out of 10

Setting Tactics Drills

1. Location setting   ___out of 10
2. Setting against the flow   ___out of 10
3. Setting against the middle   ___out of 10

    Total   **___out of 60**

Attacking

The skills of serving, passing, and setting are largely finesse skills. While certain attacks also require finesse, it is on the third contact that power comes into play. The objective of every attack is to get a *kill,* a ball that either finds the floor on the opponent's side of the net or prevents the opponent from legally making a second contact. While getting a kill is the goal of every attacker, simply forcing the opponent to handle difficult balls can result in points for your team. You can attack a ball in many ways and different situations require different techniques. Throughout this step we introduce a variety of techniques that will prepare you for every situation.

ATTACKING TECHNIQUE

The simplest way to describe attacking is as a three-step process:

1. Run to the ball.
2. Jump to the ball.
3. Throw your hand through the ball.

That may sound simple, but hitting a moving object as hard as you can while also in the air is a challenging feat. In this step, we discuss the techniques that will allow you to attack with consistency and power along with the strategies used to score points.

Approach

As with passing and setting, your movement to the ball in attacking plays an important role. Your approach develops horizontal momentum that can be transferred into a strong vertical jump, puts your torso in a position to generate torque, and facilitates your ability to reach as high as possible when contacting the ball.

The four-step approach is the best way to move to the ball for an attack. The following steps describe the four-step approach for a right-handed hitter; a left-handed hitter uses the opposite footwork.

Start a step behind the 10-foot (3 m) line facing the net with your weight on your left foot and at a 45-degree angle to where you intend to hit the ball. Take a small step toward the net with your right foot and begin to lean forward, keeping a slight bend in your knees (figure 4.1*a*). Take a larger step with your left foot and bend deeper at the knee and at the waist (figure 4.1b). Keep your arms relaxed and by your sides. Leap off your left foot and reach with your right foot so that your third step is long (figure 4.1c). When you place your right foot on the ground, point your toe toward the court and parallel to the net. While taking the third step, swing your arms and hands back and lean forward with your shoulders. Rotate your hips and plant your left foot parallel to your right foot about shoulder-width apart (figure 4.1d). Draw both arms forward and overhead as you transfer your horizontal momentum up and jump to the ball.

Figure 4.1 FOUR-STEP APPROACH (RIGHT-HANDED PLAYER)

First Step

1. Start behind 10-foot (3 m) line.
2. Face the net.
3. Put weight on left foot.
4. Stand at 45-degree angle to where ball will go.
5. Take small step with right foot and lean forward.

Second Step

1. Take a long step with left foot.
2. Bend deeper at knees and waist.
3. Keep arms relaxed by sides.

Third Step

1. Leap off left foot and take long step with right foot.
2. Point right toes toward court and right foot parallel to net.
3. Swing arms and hands back.
4. Lean forward with shoulders.

Fourth Step

1. Rotate hips and plant left foot parallel to right foot.
2. Position feet shoulder-width apart.
3. Draw arms forward and overhead.
4. Jump to the ball off two feet.

The first couple steps of your approach should be somewhat slow, but momentum should increase quickly so that the last two steps are fast. This is called a *crescendo approach* because it starts off slow with small steps and ends big and fast.

Sometimes there is not enough time or space to perform all four steps of this approach pattern. Middle hitters, for instance, might only be able to get two steps off the net before they need to begin their approach. While you may lose momentum, power, and reach, you must be able to adapt and put yourself in the best position possible to aggressively attack the ball. If you have time for only two steps, then use the last two steps to plant to the set, jump, and swing. If you have time for three, use the last three. Volleyball is a game of opportunity, not perfection, and requires players to make constant adjustments in order to get the most out of every rally.

Arm Swing

Ideally, your approach will put you in a position to contact the ball as high as possible and have many attacking options—line, angle, or off speed—with power. To achieve maximal consistency and power through the arm swing, follow these guidelines.

After you are in the air and both hands are up to reach for the ball, draw your dominant elbow back and bend the elbow so that your hand comes behind your head (figure 4.2*a*). Your elbows should be at the same height with both hands up, making a T at your shoulders. Rotate your hips and shoulders toward the opponent's court in order to add torque to your attack (figure 4.2*b*). Reach your dominant elbow to the ball and extend your hand to follow while letting your nondominant arm fall and bend naturally (you don't need to focus on this; it should do it on its own). With a large palm, drive your hand through the center of the ball while at maximum jump height, allowing your wrist to naturally snap over the ball (figure 4.2*c*). Let your hand fall back to your hip after you make contact and get into position to play defense.

Figure 4.2　ARM SWING

Draw Elbow Back

1. From last step of approach, swing both arms above head.
2. Bring dominant elbow back.
3. Bend dominant elbow so hand goes behind head.
4. Position elbows at the same height.

Rotate

1. Rotate hips and shoulders toward opponent's court.
2. Reach dominant elbow to ball.
3. Extend elbow to throw hand toward the ball.

Contact

1. Drive palm through center of ball.
2. Snap wrist naturally over ball.
3. Return hand to hip after contact.
4. Get in defensive position.

MISSTEP

You have to reach out, forward, or behind yourself to make good contact with the ball.

CORRECTION

Adjust the steps of the approach to put yourself in position to get maximal reach.

Hand Contact

Your hand contact on the ball determines where it goes. If you contact below the ball and fail to snap your hand over the top of the ball, it likely will sail deep out of bounds. If you contact on top of the ball too much, you likely will attack into the block or the net. Contacting the center of the ball with a loose and relaxed wrist (the force of the forward shoulder momentum will naturally snap the wrist when it contacts the ball) will ensure that the ball goes where you want it to go. While this is a low-error method for attacking, it also makes it easy for defenses to predict your intentions. In the next section, we will discuss ways to make your attacks more difficult to defend.

SLIDE ATTACK

A volleyball attack different from the typical two-footed approach described earlier is the slide attack (figure 4.3). The footwork pattern follows that of a basketball layup. A hitter runs to the set, plants the leg opposite her dominant arm, jumps off one foot, and drifts in the air to attack the ball. The slide approach presents interesting advantages:

- It allows the hitter to float along the net, giving her more places to hit the ball.
- It allows right-handed hitters to attack with power (generated by torso rotation) at the right antenna and left-handed hitters to do the same in front of the setter.
- It is challenging to block because it is difficult to predict where the hitter will attack.
- It provides an option for attacking at the right antenna even when the setter is in the front row.

A critical element of the slide attack is to keep the ball just in front of the body at all phases of the approach. Once the pass has just gone ahead of you toward the setter, take a step with your left foot toward the net. As the setter sets back to the right antenna, take a long stride with your right leg parallel to the net. Keeping your hands higher than your waist and your elbows bent (as if you are running), plant your left foot at a 45-degree angle to the antenna and drive your right knee and elbow up. Rotate your shoulders so that they square to where you plan to attack the ball and whip your right hand through the ball while contacting the upper right side of the ball.

MISSTEP

Because of the horizontal momentum of the slide approach, many slide hitters drive their knees out instead of up.

CORRECTION

Focus on driving the knee straight up to transfer the horizontal momentum into vertical reach. You will still float a bit but will be able to contact higher than you would otherwise.

Figure 4.3 **SLIDE ATTACK**

Preparation

1. Pass goes just ahead of you toward setter.
2. Step with left foot toward net.
3. Setter sets back to right antenna.

Plant

1. Take long stride with right leg parallel to net.
2. Keep hands higher than waist and elbows bent.
3. Plant left foot at 45-degree angle to antenna.
4. Drive right knee and elbow up.

Contact

1. Rotate shoulders and square to ball.
2. Whip hand through ball.
3. Contact upper right side of ball.

TRANSITION

When you are attacking a ball in a match, you will seldom be standing there waiting for the set. You will be coming from a position in the serve-receive pattern or coming off a defensive assignment. How you get into position to start your approach will affect your effectiveness.

The turn-and-run technique (figure 4.4) is favored over backpedaling when making the transition from a defensive position to an offensive one. Although many players keep their shoulders square to the net and backpedal to get off the net to the 10-foot (3 m) line for their approach, this approach is slow and prevents players from getting back far enough to take an aggressive approach. The following guidelines will help your transition footwork and lead to a great attack.

When transitioning off the block, land on two feet. At one time, players were taught to land on one foot to shorten the time required to take a step off the net, but because of an increase in anterior cruciate ligament (ACL) injuries, coaches have gone back to encouraging a two-footed landing. Open to the court to spot the dig. You are about to start a dead sprint for the 10-foot (3 m) line and to do that you want to be facing where you need to go. This also provides you the opportunity to evaluate the quality of the dig and whether you will have to make adjustments, for instance when a low, fast dig makes you stop your transition short to be ready to swing. Sprint to the optimal approach position. Make a quick hop to put your weight on the correct foot to start your approach (for a right-handed player, right foot if using a three-step approach and left if using a four-step approach) and square your hips to the net. Usually you will have to rotate approximately 180 degrees.

Figure 4.4 **TURN-AND-RUN TRANSITION**

Land and Turn

1. After the block, land on two feet.
2. Open to the court.

Sprint and Set

1. Sprint to the 10-foot (3 m) line.
2. Hop onto correct approach foot.
3. Square hips to net.

Attacking Drill 1   **Self-Toss**

One of the most effective ways to learn to put the arm swing and approach together is through self-toss attacking. At the 10-foot (3 m) line and with a ball in your dominant hand, toss the ball up so that it lands 1 to 2 feet (.3-.6 m) from the net. After your toss, start your approach and arm swing. Make contact with the ball with a loose, relaxed wrist to snap the ball in the direction you are facing. Work on attacking crosscourt, followed by rotating your shoulders through the ball to attack the line. After you have mastered attacking straight, work on adding the thumb-up and thumb-down shots. You should be able to accurately attack a self-tossed ball four out of five times before moving on to the next shot. When tossing the ball to slide attack, place the ball in your non-dominant hand and toss a low ball directly to your dominant hand as you plant your last step.

TO INCREASE DIFFICULTY

- Try to turn your thumb up or down on contact and cut the ball away from the direction you are facing.
- Intentionally make a bad toss and adjust your approach to get your body to the ball.

TO DECREASE DIFFICULTY

- Move farther away from the net or even to the back row.
- Have a partner toss the ball for you.

Success Check

- Finish with a strong right-left closing step.
- Draw both arms overhead.
- Throw a relaxed hand through the ball with speed.

Score Your Success

Successful straight attack (4 out of 5 attempts) = 5 points

Successful crosscourt attack (4 out of 5 attempts) = 5 points

Successful slide attack (4 out of 5 attempts) = 5 points

Your score ___

Attacking Drill 2   **Approach Stars**

Adjusting to the set with your last two steps is a skill that many great hitters have mastered. This drill allows you to focus on only the last two steps to put yourself in a position to make an aggressive swing. To start this drill, your weight should be on your left foot (right foot for a left-handed hitter), about 5 feet (1.5 m) from the net. Follow table 4.1 to put your feet in a position that will allow you to be as tall as possible when attacking.

Table 4.1 Approach Stars Drill Angles and Tosses

Degrees (hitter facing net = zero degrees)	Approach pattern	Toss or set location
0	Normal approach pattern	Directly in front of the hitter
45	Angle your step with your right foot forward and into the court.	Inside and in front of the hitter
90	Take your right step directly to the right as if you were hopping to the side.	Directly to the right of the hitter
135	Push back off your left foot and land to the back and right.	Behind and inside the hitter
180	Push directly back so you can keep the ball in front of you.	Directly behind the hitter
270	Cross your right foot over your left and close with your left foot	Directly on the hitter's left shoulder
315	Angle your approach to the left so there is a slight crossover but with continued forward movement.	In front of and to the left of the hitter

After you contact one ball, move back to the starting position for the next ball in the series until you have gone all the way through. After you are comfortable with the last two steps, complete the same pattern using a full approach.

TO INCREASE DIFFICULTY

- Use a full approach.
- Try to place your attack to more challenging locations on the court.

TO DECREASE DIFFICULTY

- Work on the footwork without a ball.
- Throw a tennis ball across the net before hitting a volleyball.

Success Check

- Focus on a strong right-left closing step in your approach.
- Keep your shoulders open to the ball.
- Throw a loose, relaxed hand through the ball.

Score Your Success

5 or more attacks into the court with power = 10 points

3 or 4 attacks into the court with power or 5 or more attacks into the court with little power = 5 points

2 or fewer attacks into the court = 1 point

Your score ___

Attacking Drill 3   **Instructor's Toss With Transition**

With the instructor tossing from the setting location, practice attacking and transitioning at all locations. Use a slow-to-fast, four-step approach and a T-position arm swing through your hand and through the ball at maximum reach. Land on two feet and turn to run back to the 10-foot (3 m) line. Repeat three times, hitting to the same location each time. After you have gained consistency in attacking to a specific location, try to attack to different locations with each swing. When you have mastered that, shift to different locations on the net and hit four balls across the front row.

TO INCREASE DIFFICULTY

- Change the tempo of each toss.
- Change the location on the net of each attack.
- Attack each ball to a different location.

TO DECREASE DIFFICULTY

- Slow the time between tosses to allow proper transition.
- Attack every ball to the same location.

Success Check

- Use a slow-to-fast approach.
- Use a T-position arm swing.
- Use turn-and-run transition footwork.

Score Your Success

Earn 1 point for each successful attack (10 attempts).

Your score ___

ATTACKING TACTICS

Using the techniques explained in the previous sections will allow you to attack with consistency and power, but it will also make your attack easy to read by the defense. Once you develop the ability to consistently control the accuracy of your attacks, you will have the opportunity to work on deception. After all, a kill doesn't need to be a thunderous attack landing in front of the 10-foot (3 m) line. A thumb-up, thumb-down, or off-speed attack may be just what you need to keep your opponent's defense off-balance.

Attacking Straight

Following the steps described previously for the four-step approach and contacting the center of the ball will allow you to attack directly where your shoulders are facing. To attack the line, rotate your torso so that your shoulders are square to the line immediately before contact. To attack crosscourt, rotate your torso so that your shoulders are square to the crosscourt. The crosscourt attack is the safest place to attack and the place with the lowest error rate because you have the most court available to you. This attack strategy is recommended when you have a strong block in front of you or when the set is not perfect.

Thumb Up or Thumb Down

Manipulating your hand contact on the ball can deceive the defense by making the ball travel in a direction to which you are not squared. To make the ball veer to the left of where you are squared, execute the approach and arm swing as described previously, but instead of contacting the center of the ball, turn your thumb up as you make contact with the right side of the ball (figure 4.5a). To make the ball veer to the right, turn your thumb down as you make contact with the left side of the ball (figure 4.5b). Because this is a more challenging attack, hold your extension without following through until you are comfortable swinging all the way through the ball.

Figure 4.5   Change the hand contact on the ball: (a) turn your thumb up to make the ball veer to the left; (b) turn your thumb down to make the ball veer to the right.

Off-Speed Attacks

Open-hand tips are attacks that contact the ball softly with the fingertips (figure 4.6a) and direct it to an open area of the court, usually shallow and close to the blockers. For a roll shot (figure 4.6b), drop your elbow just before contact to get your full hand under the ball. Snapping your wrist then forces the ball into an upward trajectory short over the block and deep into the opponent's backcourt. Tips and roll shots are referred to as off-speed attacks because, like a changeup pitch in baseball, they are shots that catch the defenders off guard and out of rhythm.

Figure 4.6   Off-speed attacks: *(a)* open-hand tip, and *(b)* roll shot.

MISSTEP

You give away your off-speed shot by dropping your elbow early or by slowing your approach.

CORRECTION

Try to make your off-speed approach and arm swing look as much like your full approach and arm swing for as long as possible.

Attacking Quick Sets

When you have developed a trusting relationship with your setter, attacking quick sets can be effective. A quick set is one in which the setter sets directly to the hitter's reach instead of lofting the ball high and letting the hitter approach the ball. Quick sets require timing and trust between a hitter and a setter because the hitter approaches to the place the ball will be set and not to where he or she sees the ball going. To execute a quick set, adjust your approach so that you stay with the pass as it goes toward the setter. Plant your feet and jump just as the setter makes contact with his or her hands and draw your arm swing back quickly to give your setter a target location to set to (figure 4.7).

Attacking quick sets are much more successful when the pass is perfect because the depth and distance of the set is consistent. When the pass is imperfect, set depth and distance are adjusted to create an angle that allows the hitter to open his or her shoulders to the setter. The attacker should approach as far away from the setter as the setter is off the net. When the pass is perfect, the

Figure 4.7 Hitter setting the target for a quick set.

hitter should approach to the location just in front of the setter. When the pass pulls the setter 8 feet (2.4 m) off the net, the hitter should approach to a location 8 feet away from the setter at a 45-degree angle to the net (figure 4.8). By increasing the space between the setter and hitter on imperfect passes, the angle widens and allows the hitter to have a better view of the set as it comes to her. The speed of the set should remain the same.

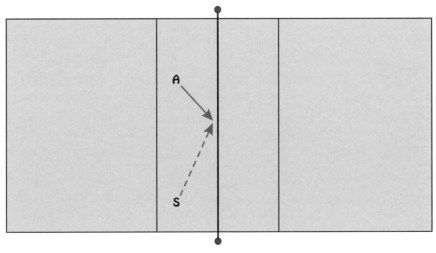

Figure 4.8 Positions of the hitter and setter during a quick set.

Back-Row Attacking

When attacking from the back row, it is important to adjust your plant and jump so that you are slightly more under the ball when you make contact. Because you are farther away from the net, the ball must take a flatter trajectory as it crosses into the opponent's court. Strike the ball with maximal velocity and wrist snap to add topspin.

Attacking From the Right Antenna

The attacking steps covered in this step are generally accurate regardless of where you attack from and whether you are left- or right-handed. The challenge of being a right-handed attacker on the right side is that your plant foot (the last step of your approach) faces the opposite direction of where the ball comes from. When this happens, start your approach slightly inside the court and approach straight to the net (0 degrees instead of 45). While you will give up the potential to generate power, the benefit of making a more consistent contact on the ball is worth the sacrifice.

Second-Contact Attacking

Just because the rules allow three contacts on your side before you send the ball to your opponent does not mean that you have to use them. Setters typically are the highest-efficiency hitters on the court because it is difficult to defend a setter's dump to the middle of the court as well as a hitter's attack deep in the court. To attack the second contact, jump and square up to your hitter as if you were going to set to the hitter. Just before contact, pull your right hand down and use your left hand to direct the ball over the net. The most vulnerable spot on the opponent's floor is usually the middle of the court. Because the dump is usually a slower attack, you want to place it shallow in the court to minimize the defense's reaction time. A left-handed setter has the advantage because she can use an approach and arm swing to attack the second contact (which is why many setters are left-handed), but that should not stop right-handed setters from considering the option. Here are strategies for being an offensive setter:

- Use the dump sparingly because its effectiveness comes through the element of surprise.
- Use the setter dump in the later stages of a rally and not when the opponent's defense is set up and waiting for it.
- Use the setter dump in combination with other quick attacks to confuse blockers and force them to jump when you jump.
- Jump set balls to both antennae and the middles so that you don't give away your intention to attack simply by leaving the ground.
- When teams adjust to the shallow tip, attack the ball deep to the corners. No team can cover the *entire* court.

Attacking Tactics Drill 1
Location Attacking (Angles and Depth)

Practice attacking to different locations off an instructor's toss from both the right and left sides. When your accuracy to different areas becomes consistent, work on your contact point on the ball to send it to various depths. Set up cones designating the back 5 feet (1.5 m) of the court from your attacking location. Set up another set of cones 3 feet (1 m) in front of that. Contact below the ball to send it deep in the court or on top to attack down in front of diggers. After consistently hitting each depth successively, alternate between the two.

TO INCREASE DIFFICULTY

- Have a setter set instead of using an instructor's toss.
- Make the target areas smaller.
- Provide sets that are more challenging to attack to the target area (when attacking the line, toss the ball too far inside).
- Work on deception by facing one way and hitting another (thumb down).
- Use a slide approach when attacking a ball at the right antenna.

TO DECREASE DIFFICULTY

- Make target areas larger.
- Keep sets off the net.

Success Check

- Use a slow-to-fast approach.
- Change your hand contact for more control.
- Face the direction you are attacking.

Score Your Success

Earn 1 point for each successful attack deep to the opponent's court and shallow to the opponent's court from both the right and left antennae (5 attempts each).

Your score ___

Attacking Tactics Drill 2   **Inside or Outside**

This is a 4v4 scrimmage that uses the outside lines of the court and lines created by cones that sit inside the middle of the court, creating a square 10 feet × 10 feet (3 m × 3 m) (figure 4.9). At the start of each rally, the instructor calls out either "inside" or "outside" before initiating play with a free ball. The call corresponds to the area of the court that is in bounds. If the instructor calls "inside," the 10 × 10 square is the only area of the court that is inbounds, and teams should try to attack the middle of the court. If the instructor calls "outside," the 10 × 10 square is out of bounds. Use hand control accuracy to attack to the appropriate area of the court and keep your wits about you so that you know what is in and what is out; it can change anytime the instructor chooses. Play until a team scores 10 points or for a specific amount of time.

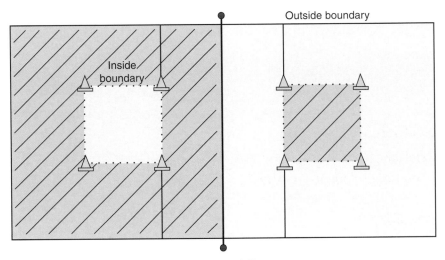

Figure 4.9   Court setup for inside-or-outside drill.

TO INCREASE DIFFICULTY

- Change the inside-outside call in the middle of the rally.

TO DECREASE DIFFICULTY

- Keep the inside-outside call consistent for three consecutive rallies.
- Change the size of the inside square to make it larger and easier to attack into.

Success Check

- Communicate throughout the rally.
- Plant to the ball so that you have multiple attacking options.
- Contact the center of the ball to ensure accuracy.

Score Your Success

Your team wins the game = 10 points

Your team loses the game = number of points the team earned

Your score ___

Attacking Tactics Drill 3
In- and Out-of-System Quick Attacking

The objective of this drill is to develop a relationship between the middle hitter and setter so that they can remain a viable offensive threat even when the pass is off the net. Take a long piece of elastic (you can use the same piece used in the serving step) and tie it to the poles on both sides of the net at the height of the setter's waist. The setter takes position between the net and the elastic. As the setter comes off the net to get to a pass tossed by the instructor, the elastic creates a triangle. The elastic provides a guide so the hitter knows how far away from the net to stay. Ideally, the hitter approaches a position that is as far away from the setter, at a 45-degree angle, as the setter is off the net. Make sure the hitter continues to square up to the setter in order to stay open to the set. Attack the ball to the back corners of the court.

TO INCREASE DIFFICULTY

- The instructor tosses the ball to the setter faster.
- The instructor tosses to the setter farther off the net.
- The hitter uses a slide approach and a back set from the setter.

TO DECREASE DIFFICULTY

- The instructor keeps the tosses closer to the setter's spot.
- The coach tosses higher to give the hitter time to adjust.

Success Check

- Square up to your setter.
- Stay off the net.
- Keep your attacking elbow high.

Score Your Success

As the hitter, earn 1 point every time you correctly set up in relation to the setter (10 attempts).

Your score ___

Attacking Tactics Drill 4 **Redemption**

With a front-row setter and three back-row players on each side of the net, initiate a free ball to side A. Side A gets three contacts to play the ball to the opposing side. Attackers should work on attacking with consistency, but if they make a mistake, the instructor gives them an opportunity to redeem themselves by tossing a ball similar to the ball on which they erred. If they keep that ball in play, the rally continues, but if they make a second mistake, they are replaced by other players. This drill teaches players how to take risks, but not make the same mistake twice. The instructor can give redemption opportunities on any type of ball, including attacking a ball at a defender when he misses a dig. Every time a player is replaced, a point is added to the team's score. A game lasts five minutes.

TO INCREASE DIFFICULTY

- Make the redemption opportunity more challenging.
- Require a push-up or squat jump between redemption opportunities.

TO DECREASE DIFFICULTY

- Allow players to make two or more errors, but not the same type of error twice.

Success Check

- Take an aggressive crescendo approach.
- Aim for the greatest amount of available court on the opponent's side.
- Swing with confidence.

Score Your Success

Your team finishes with fewer than 3 points = 10 points

Your team finishes with 4 to 7 points = 5 points

Your team finishes with 7 points or more = 1 point

Your score ___

SUCCESS SUMMARY

Using an aggressive approach, an arm swing that employs a high and fast-hitting hand, and a relaxed wrist snapping through the ball, you can crush kills all over the court! These fundamentals allow you to attack with power, accuracy, and deception. Whether using a standard four-step approach, running a slide, or attacking in transition, it is imperative that you get your body to the ball to maximize your reach and make your hand contact as fast as you can make it. When you feel confident in your ability to perform these skills and have earned 60 points in the drills, you are ready to take the next step to blocking.

Attacking Drills

1. Self-toss   ___out of 15

2. Approach stars   ___out of 10

3. Instructor's toss with transition   ___out of 10

Attacking Tactics Drills

1. Location attacking (angles and depth)   ___out of 20

2. Inside or outside   ___out of 10

3. In- and out-of-system quick attacking   ___out of 10

4. Redemption   ___out of 10

   Total   **___out of 85**

Blocking

Analysis of the techniques used in any sport will reveal a range of successful approaches. Volleyball is no different. Players can learn many effective ways to serve, pass, set, and attack, and this book shares with you the approach that is easiest to learn and leads to quick success.

At the collegiate and international levels of play, the skill of blocking might be the easiest skill in which to identify clear differences in technique between high-achieving performers. Regardless of how you go about executing this skill, blocking has three main goals:

1. Prevent the opponent's attack from crossing the net into your defense.
2. Channel the opponent's attack to your best diggers.
3. Take away your opponent's most effective attack.

You can reach these objectives in multiple ways, and this step identifies the techniques that will help you to do this consistently and successfully.

BLOCKING TECHNIQUE

Blocking with strength takes discipline and explosiveness. There is a lot to do and very little time to do it in when blocking a good offensive team. Following certain technical cues will help you to not just block more balls but also facilitate the success of your defense when you don't get the block.

Base Position

Your starting position as a blocker should be with your body close to the net (1 to 2 feet [.3-.6 m] away), the weight on the balls of your feet, your knees slightly bent, and your hands at head level with your elbows in (figure 5.1). This position is compact enough that you are able to move quickly but not so compact that you are unable to quickly get your hands over the net if necessary.

Figure 5.1 **BLOCKING START POSITION**

1. Stand with body close to net.
2. Weight is on balls of feet.
3. Knees are slightly bent.
4. Hands are at chin level, elbows in.

MISSTEP

You are squared to the setter and stay with him, but you are not far enough in front of him.

CORRECTION

Start your base blocking position all the way in front of the setter in order to successfully block the attack to the middle of the court, the most vulnerable place on the court in most defenses.

Eye Sequencing

The most often overlooked element of blocking technique is the activity of the eyes when the ball is on the opponent's side of the net. The first cue to look at is the pass. When the pass is poor, the opposing setter might not be able to get your hitter the ball. In these situations, you can leave your hitter and help a blocker whose hitter is more likely to be set.

The next cue is to watch the setter and identify where he or she is setting. You might be able to read the setter's posture or hand placement on the ball and get an early jump on which attacker is being set. After the ball has been set, identify whether or not the ball is being set tight or off the net. When the ball is set tight, try to surround the ball with your hands and jump with the hitter. When the ball is set off the net, read your hitter and jump after she jumps, because of the time it takes the ball to get to the net.

Finally, your attention will leave the ball and focus directly on the hitter. Because the hitter has to make contact with the ball, you can trust that her body position will tell you where the ball is. Focus your eyes on the hitter's body placement and arm swing so that you properly align your hands against her attack (figure 5.2).

Figure 5.2 Proper alignment of the hands against the attack.

MISSTEP

You watch the pass and set too long.

CORRECTION

After you can predict the set distance and depth of the pass or set, redirect your attention to the next appropriate cue. Some coaches have their blockers wear visors or baseball caps to keep their eyes level and prevent them from watching the pass and set for the entire duration.

Footwork

As one of three blockers across the front row covering a 29-foot, 6-inch (9 m) net, each player is responsible for about 10 feet (3 m) of the net. Most people are not able to cover that by simply jumping to position; thus, proper footwork helps the blocker get to position on balance and with maximal jump potential. Three footwork patterns can be used to cover the distance necessary to get into a position to block.

STEP CLOSE

When you have to make small adjustments (1 to 2 feet [.3-.6 m]) with your block placement, take a side step in the direction that you need to go with the nearest foot and push off with the opposite foot. For instance, if you are blocking on the right side and the set is pushed out past your position, hop to the right by pushing off your left foot and reaching with your right. You should land on both feet almost simultaneously and with a deep knee bend in order to explode immediately on the jump (figure 5.3).

Figure 5.3 STEP-CLOSE FOOTWORK

1. Side step with nearest foot.
2. Push off with other foot.
3. Land on both feet.
4. Bend knees deeply.

CROSSOVER CLOSE

Sometimes you need to move along the net a little farther than one hop step will take you. To travel 3 to 5 feet (1-1.5 m), start by crossing the foot farthest from the direction that you are traveling over the other foot (figure 5.4). Execute the step close as described previously in order to properly align your body with your attacker.

Figure 5.4 **CROSSOVER-CLOSE FOOTWORK**

1. Cross outside foot over inside foot.
2. Side step with inside foot.
3. Push off with outside foot.
4. Land on both feet.
5. Bend knees deeply.

STEP-CROSSOVER CLOSE

An additional step is required when trying to travel 6 to 10 feet (1.8-3 m) along the net. Initiate the footwork by taking a small step in the direction you want to move with the foot closest to that direction (figure 5.5). Bending at the waist slightly and moving your center of gravity in that direction while taking the step will add momentum that can help you extend the length of the crossover-close steps. Your hands should stay near your head while you are moving and your hips should rotate only 45 degrees from the opposing court. This blocking footwork is primarily used by players starting in the middle to get to the antennae and establish a strong double block.

Figure 5.5 **STEP-CROSSOVER-CLOSE FOOTWORK**

1. Take small step with outside foot.
2. Bend slightly at waist.
3. Open shoulders to antenna.
4. Leap with the outside foot toward hitter.
5. Push off with outside foot.
6. Land on both feet squared to the hitter.
7. Bend knees deeply.
8. Keep hands near head.

Block Timing

Several factors influence when to jump to block. For most situations, you want to initiate your block jump immediately after the hitter has initiated his approach jump. On occasion, adjustments to this rule are required. Most important in knowing when to jump is understanding how far off the net the ball is being set. The farther off the net, the longer the blocker needs to wait because the ball will take longer to get from the attacker's hands to the blocker's hands. Another factor influencing the timing of the block is your vertical jump in comparison to the attacker's vertical jump. If the attacker can reach significantly higher than you can, it is wise to jump after the hitter so that you both reach maximum height at the same time.

MISSTEP

You jump laterally to line up in the air.

CORRECTION

Blockers should always jump straight up without floating right or left, even if it means they are poorly aligned with the block. Reaching with your hands and jumping laterally makes you weaker and increases your chances of making a poor block deflection.

Hands Presentation

After you have planted with bent knees and are ready to jump, extend your elbows completely overhead. Turn your thumbs to the ceiling so that your fingers take up more horizontal space (figure 5.6a). When your fingertips get higher than the top of the net, begin to press your hands through the plane created by the net into the opponent's court. Round your shoulders forward to use additional shoulder muscles to stabilize your block as you continue to reach forward for the ball. As your hands cross the plane of the net, they should angle down. Contract your core muscles as the ball hits your arms (figure 5.6b) in order to make sure the ball rebounds and returns to your opponent's court. After you have reached the peak of your jump and are returning to the court, keep your arms extended and land on two feet (figure 5.6c).

Figure 5.6 **BLOCKING WITH THE HANDS**

Preparation

1. Get ready to jump.
2. Extend elbows.
3. Turn thumbs to ceiling.

Execution

1. Jump.
2. Press hands through plane of net into opponent's court.
3. Round shoulders forward.
4. Reach for ball.
5. Angle hands down.
6. Hit ball.

Follow-Through

1. Keep arms extended.
2. Land on two feet.
3. Get back to starting position to prepare for next block or prepare to attack.

If the block was successful, get back to your starting position and prepare to block again. If the opposing hitter avoided your block and attacked the ball to your back-court, land, turn your body open to the court, and run 10 feet (3 m) off the net to be ready as an attacker. If the ball touches your block but continues onto your side of the net, the contact does not count against your three available contacts, and you can contact it again.

MISSTEP

You try to reach as high as possible without reaching over into the opponent's court.

CORRECTION

When you reach over the net, your hands take up more court space than they otherwise would, and a blocked ball is more likely to go to the opponent's floor than land on your side of the net.

Soft Blocking

Are you worried that when you block, you cannot reach all the way over the net? A player can still be an effective blocker even when he lacks either the height or vertical jump to get higher than the net. The technique of soft blocking employs the same footwork and hand presentation techniques described previously, with one important difference. Instead of reaching your hands over the net into the opponent's court, tilt your hands back so that your palms face the ceiling (figure 5.7). Be sure that both hands are as flat as possible. You won't get many block kills with this technique, but you will touch a lot more balls that hitters would have otherwise been able to hit over you. Touching the ball should slow it enough that it becomes an easy attack for your back row to pass. Soft blocking can be especially frustrating to a hitter if she feels like she should be more successful because of the mismatch in height or jump.

Figure 5.7 Hand position for a soft block.

Swing Blocking

Swing blocking involves exchanging the step-crossover-close footwork with an approach similar to attacking. By starting your base position inside and using a dynamic approach and arm swing, you will be able to cover more of the net, jump higher, time your block with the hitter, and easily engage your whole core to block (figure 5.8). As the number of moving parts increases, so does the complexity of the skill. Swing blocking can take a long time to master, but follow these steps to become more comfortable with the technique.

Your base position is on the net about 10 feet from the antenna. Open your hips and shoulders to the direction you want to travel. Start your footwork when the hitter starts his approach. Use a three-step approach (left-right-left if moving to the left and right-left-right if moving to the right) similar to attacking. Swing your arms the same way you would when attacking but bend the elbows. This makes the lever shorter and limits net violations when you bring your arms forward. As you plant your feet to jump, rotate your hips back to the court so that they are squared to your attacker. Throw your hands up to the ball and reach back into the court to help close the block with the middle blocker. Keep your arms extended and hips square as you return to the ground.

Figure 5.8 **SWING BLOCK**

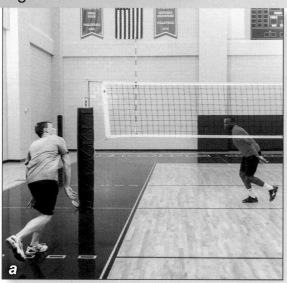

Preparation

1. Stand on net about 10 feet (3 m) from antenna.
2. Open hips and shoulders.
3. When hitter starts to approach, use three-step approach.
4. Swing arms with elbows bent.

Execution

1. Plant feet.
2. Rotate hips to court to square with attacker.
3. Lift hands to ball and reach back into court to close block.

Follow-Through

1. Keep arms extended.
2. Keep hips square.
3. Land on ground.

Blocking Technique Drill 1   **Partner Blocking**

Standing on the ground, partners face each other approximately 2 feet (.6 m) apart. One player tosses a ball while her partner presents her hands to block. Focus on full elbow extension, thumbs pointed to the ceiling, and a strong core. The attacking partner uses a good arm swing technique to attack the ball against the outstretched hands of her partner. Be sure the blocker's fingers are pointed up and that the ball is not hit down at the fingers (possible if the hitter is taller than the blocker). The blocker should contract her abdominal muscles and press the ball downward. The ball should rebound off the blocker's hands and go straight to the floor. Perform the drill 10 times and switch roles.

TO INCREASE DIFFICULTY

- Try attacking off one hand more than the other.
- Add a slight hop as the blocker.
- Make the blocker balance on an unstable surface (like a BOSU or balance cushion).

TO DECREASE DIFFICULTY

- Hit squarely into the blocker's hands.
- Attack softly.

Success Check

- Focus on full elbow extension.
- Keep thumbs pointed to the ceiling.
- Keep a strong core.

Score Your Success

Earn 1 point for each successful block (10 attempts).

Your score ___

Blocking Technique Drill 2   **Blind Blocking**

It is important for the blocker to focus on watching the assigned hitter instead of watching the ball. For this drill, players are divided into groups of three (one attacker, one tosser, and one blocker) and the entire court is divided into two lanes. The attacker is on one side of the net with a tosser and blocker on the other side. The blocker faces the attacker, and the tosser is behind the blocker (figure 5.9). The tosser gently lobs the ball 2 to 3 feet (.6-1 m) over the net so that the attacker can approach and hit the ball. The blocker, with her back to the toss, is forced to focus on the attacker's approach pattern and line up appropriately on the attacker's arm. The attacker facilitates the blocker's success by attacking directly into the blocker's hands. Perform the drill 10 times and then rotate responsibilities, keeping track of the number of successful blocks.

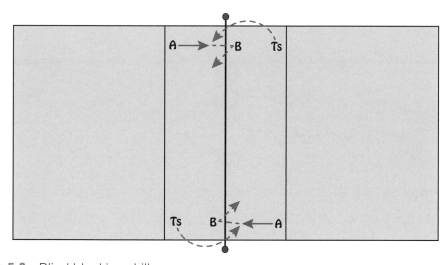

Figure 5.9 Blind blocking drill.

TO INCREASE DIFFICULTY

- Toss the ball so that the attacker makes contact farther away from the net.
- Toss the ball to the side to force the blocker to step to the side.
- Tell the attacker to try to hit the ball off one hand or a fingertip.

TO DECREASE DIFFICULTY

- Toss the ball tighter so that the attacker has very little room to swing around the block.

Success Check

- Watch your hitter, not the ball.
- Jump immediately after your hitter.
- Press on the block with your core.

Score Your Success

Earn 1 point for each successful block (10 attempts) plus half a point for every blocking point of the others in your group.

Your score ___

Blocking Technique Drill 3 **Outsides vs. Blockers**

Position three left-side hitters and a setter on one side of the net. On the other side of the net stand two right-side blockers and two middles. The coach tosses the ball to the setter, who sets the first left side hitter in line. As the set is made, the middle blocker uses the step-crossover-close footwork to close to the right-side blocker. Hitters should attack into the blocker's hands. When 10 balls have been attacked, setters and hitters switch roles with the blockers and repeat. Keep track of the number of blocked balls.

TO INCREASE DIFFICULTY

- Have hitters attack vulnerable places in the block (the seam between blockers, the outside hand of the pin blocker).

TO DECREASE DIFFICULTY

- Have attackers hit a ball tossed by an instructor.
- Set the ball tighter to the net.

Success Check

- Blockers should have four hands together squared to the court.
- Watch your hitter.
- Keep arms extended until you land.

Score Your Success

Earn 1 point for each successful block (10 attempts) plus a half point for every successful block that you hit into.

Your score ___

BLOCKING TACTICS

Your team can use multiple blocking strategies. Some strategies focus on stopping opposing middle hitters and quick sets, while others focus on slowing hitters at the antennae. Some teams let their blockers read the opponent's setter and wait to close the block until the set has been released, while others will set up their block early to try to influence where the setter will send the ball. All blocking strategies carry with them advantages and challenges, but carefully choosing a tactic helps to make sure all teammates understand its purpose.

Spread vs. Bunch Blocking

Your base position as a blocker is determined by the blocking strategy your team has chosen. When spread blocking, the pin blockers start an arm's length from the antenna, and the middle blocker is in the middle of the court. The middle remains there when bunch blocking, but the pins move in to help with a quick middle attack. Spread blocking is advantageous when your opponent attacks mostly from the outside positions or if you intend to block the line.

Bunch blocking is when the left- and right-side blockers stand an arm's length away from the middle. This strategy provides more opportunity to double block a quick offense in the middle as well as more room for swing blocking. You can compare the two types of blocking in figure 5.10.

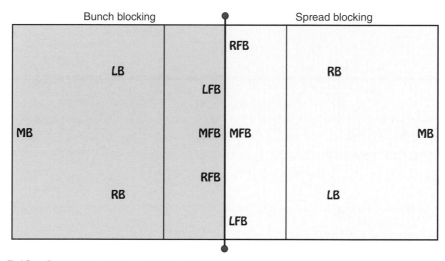

Figure 5.10   Spread and bunch blocking.

These positions sometimes change when the setter is front row. Because the offensive setter is able to quickly attack the ball with his or her left hand, it is important for the left-side blocker to front the setter, which means to take a position in front of the setter so that the left-side blocker is in the setter's view when looking forward.

MISSTEP

You stay squared to the setter and stay with him but are not far enough in front of him.

CORRECTION

Start your base blocking position all the way in front of the setter in order to successfully block the attack to the middle of the court, the most vulnerable place on the court in most defenses.

Taking Line and Angle

Remember that only one of the objectives of blocking includes blocking the ball back to the opponent's court for a kill. The other two objectives involve lining up the block to expose a specific area of the court where you have a strong defender or taking away the hitter's most effective shot. If you are trying to take away the line from an opponent's hitter, you want to align your inside arm on the hitter's attacking arm (figure 5.11a). For instance, if you are blocking a right-handed, left-side hitter at the right antenna, you want to position yourself so that your left arm is on the hitter's right arm. Likewise, if you are trying to take away the line from a left-handed hitter at the left antenna, you want to position yourself so that your right arm is on the hitter's left arm. To take away the crosscourt angle from a hitter, line up your outside arm on the hitter's attacking arm (figure 5.11b).

Regardless of blocking line or angle, the middle blocker always closes the block to the blocker on the outside even if the outside blocker makes a mistake. Most teams block angle, taking away the crosscourt shot, because it means the middle blocker has to travel less net to close the block, and it forces the hitter to attack an area of the court that is smaller and more difficult to attack.

Blockers at the antenna must make sure that their outside hands are turned into the court in order to keep the ball from ricocheting off their hands and out of bounds. Many hitters try to use a block intentionally to score a point.

Figure 5.11 Taking line and angle: *(a)* To take away the line from the opponent's hitter, align your inside arm with the hitter's attacking arm and *(b)* to take away the crosscourt angle, align your outside arm on the hitter's attacking arm.

MISSTEP

The pin blocker makes an alignment mistake and the middle tries to block what was supposed to be taken away. This leaves a seam in the block and is more difficult for the back row.

CORRECTION

The middle should close the block even if the outside hitter makes a mistake so that the diggers have a solid block to play around.

Closing the Block

Four hands in front of a hitter take up twice as much space as two and can significantly reduce the court space available to the attacker. If you are playing the middle position, it is your job to block with those who are blocking at the antennae. The challenge to closing a block is getting as close to the outside blocker as possible without giving the hitter a seam through which to hit. In this situation, the outside blocker is the player who sets the block, and the middle blocker closes the block (figure 5.12). Use the footwork patterns described previously to get your feet directly next to your teammate's feet and jump in unison. Synchronizing this skill takes time and communication, but when it is executed well, the ability of the defense to keep the attack off the floor significantly increases.

Figure 5.12 Double block.

Solo vs. Double Blocking

Middle blockers work hard throughout the game in order to close as many blocks as possible, but sometimes the offense is so quick that the middle cannot get out to the pin blocker. The first thing the middle must do in this situation is call "late!" to her teammate at the antenna. This will let the pin blocker know that she is going to be solo blocking the hitter. In most solo-blocking situations, it is recommended to take away the crosscourt angle even if it was earlier decided to take away the line. Most hitters can hit crosscourt much harder than they can hit line. Bringing the block inside also helps the middle when she is late to get closed. Coordinating digging responsibilities in these situations will be covered in step 8 on team defense.

MISSTEP

When a middle thinks she is going to be late to close a block, she gives up and watches the ball being set while standing at the net.

CORRECTION

Even if you cannot get all the way out to your pin blocker, get as far as you can and jump straight up as the hitter is attacking the ball, leaving a seam. Your diggers will be able to read into the seam and you might still get a block if the attacker mis-hits the ball.

Triple Blocking

We have covered how you should attempt to double block a ball set to the pins, but what if the opponent sets a high ball to the middle? In this situation, the middle blocker would set the alignment of the block by stepping in front of the approaching attacker, and the pin blockers would close to the middle using the footwork and hand positioning described previously (figure 5.13). Some teams choose not to triple block the middle attack, even when they can, simply because it leaves the backcourt vulnerable to tips. This is a decision you will have to make as you consider the shots available to the hitters you are competing against.

Figure 5.13   Triple block.

Jousting

A joust happens when the ball is in the plane of the net and simultaneously contacted by players from both teams. The joust is challenging because three forces are at play—the ball's path, the opponent's force, and your force—and they can interact unpredictably. The following are keys to winning jousts, and some players have the skills to consistently use the forces at play to their advantage:

- Be stronger than your opponent. Use your core to exert more force on the ball to prevent the ball from coming down on your side of the net.

- Be slightly late to the contact. The second person to touch the ball in a joust usually wins because she will be earlier in her force production. The counterforce applied by the second contact disrupts the initial force after some of it is already spent.

- Finish the contact at an angle. Use your wrists to redirect the ball to the right or left so that the defense cannot easily make a play on it.

Being proficient at winning jousts might help your team score only a few more points each match. However, because your team trusts you to win balls that are passed tight to the net, it makes your teammates more comfortable taking the risk of passing tighter and facilitates a faster offense.

Blocking Tactics Drill 1
Oklahoma Drill (Hitting and Blocking)

This drill is named after the one-on-one football drill developed at the University of Oklahoma. This two-person drill allows the blocker to work on adjusting the block to take away the line or angle and allows the hitter to work on avoiding the block.

Divide the entire court into two lanes across the net. You and your partner work in only one lane (figure 5.14). Face your partner, who will self-toss attack on the other side of the net. Choose to block either angle or line and line up appropriately after your partner's toss. Your partner can start off by attacking into your block to test your strength and technique, but eventually the hitter should try to avoid your block and make the ball land inbounds in your lane. The attacker hits 10 balls then switches roles.

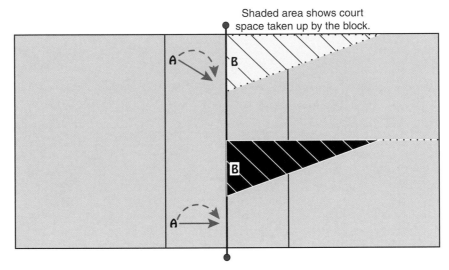

Figure 5.14   Oklahoma drill.

 TO INCREASE DIFFICULTY

- Attacker varies the depth of her toss to challenge the blocker's timing.
- Attacker uses thumb up or thumb down to make it more difficult to read the attack.

 TO DECREASE DIFFICULTY

- Attack into the blocker.
- Toss tighter to the net.
- Decrease the court space for the attacker to hit into.

Success Check

- Watch your hitter.
- Stay disciplined in your blocking alignment. Don't reach.
- Land with arms extended and squared to the court.

Earn 2 points for each successful block and 1 point for each ball that lands in the exposed area of the court (10 attempts).

Your score ____

Blocking Tactics Drill 2   Front Row vs. Front Row

To get better at blocking a combination of hitters, place three players in the front row on both sides of the net and place a back-row setter. A coach or player tosses a ball to the setter on side A, who then sets to a teammate and attacks the ball to side B. Side B attempts a solid double block. They then transition off to the 10-foot (3 m) line to receive the toss from the coach on side B to the setter and attack to side A. Each team gets a point when their block includes a closed middle blocker and both blockers landing on balance. Play to 10 points. Eventually add a point to the offense for attacking the ball into the open court (no off-speed shots) and a point to the blockers for getting the block.

TO INCREASE DIFFICULTY

- Have hitters avoid the block.
- Have hitters run crossing plays (explained in step 7).
- Speed up the drill by tossing a ball to the opposite setter immediately after the ball is attacked.

TO DECREASE DIFFICULTY

- Have hitters attack into block.
- Slow the drill to provide more transition time.

Success Check

- Read the opponent's setter.
- Close the block by getting hip to hip.
- Watch the hitter, not the ball.
- Land on balance.

Score Your Success

Your team wins = 10 points

Opponent wins = number of points your team earned

Your score ____

Blocking Tactics Drill 3   **Joust Rally Start**

Begin with six players on each side of the net in base positions. The coach starts each rally by tossing a ball on top of the net for players to joust. Play continues if the team that loses the joust can keep the ball off the floor. Play three rallies, with each front-row player getting the opportunity to go for the joust and then switch front-row and back-row players. Try to match up players across the net from each other who are of similar height.

TO INCREASE DIFFICULTY

- The instructor initiates the rally by tossing the ball to one side off the net and forces the blocker to decide whether she should joust or pass to the setter.
- Test the defense by having the instructor toss a surprise ball to them instead of the blockers.

TO DECREASE DIFFICULTY

- The instructor keeps the toss short so that it is easier to time.
- The instructor tells which two blockers will get the toss.

Success Check

- Finish the contact at an angle.
- Be slightly late to the contact.
- Be stronger than your opponent.

Score Your Success

Your team wins more jousts = 10 points

The other team wins more jousts = 5 points

Your score ___

SUCCESS SUMMARY

Blocking may not score many points for your team, but a well-formed block can make it much easier to play defense behind it. Reading the play, using the proper footwork, presenting strong and squared hands, and landing on balance are critical to establishing a formidable block as well as giving your diggers something to read around. Continue to work on pressing into your opponent's court because your block is most effective when your hands are closest to your hitter's contact. If you can't get over the net, you can still be an effective blocker by soft blocking and slowing your opponent's attacks. Once you feel confident in your blocking skills and have amassed 60 points in the drills, you can take the next step toward understanding digging.

Blocking Technique Drills

1. Partner blocking   ___ out of 10

2. Blind blocking   ___ out of 20

3. Outsides vs. blockers   ___ out of 15

Blocking Tactics Drills

1. Oklahoma drill (hitting and blocking)   ___ out of 20

2. Front row vs. front row   ___ out of 10

3. Joust rally start   ___ out of 10

   Total   **___ out of 85**

Digging

When the blockers are unable to stop the attack, it is time for the back row of the defense to keep the ball from hitting the floor. One of the beautiful aspects of volleyball is the combination of power and finesse, and nowhere are those characteristics more present than in the skill of digging. Effective back-row defense requires quickness, balance, aggressiveness, and touch; these defenders must be able to dive for balls that are attacked at 70 miles per hour (113 km/h) and then crash into the floor after making contact with the ball. Technical excellence and an understanding of the defensive plan are coupled with fearlessness and drive to make strong back-row diggers. They may not get the glory and praise offered to the top attackers on a team, but their importance and influence on the game is unquestioned. In this step, we break down the techniques used by back-row players as well as the unique challenges of digging from different positions in the back row.

DIGGING TECHNIQUES

Digging requires an explosive and strong ready position, quick footwork, and platform control, but the most overlooked digging skill is the ability to read the opponent. Every hitter provides subtle hints that give away where he will attack. As you become more experienced, you will pick up on these tells just like a savvy poker player can tell when someone is bluffing. In the meantime, practicing these skill cues will help you react quickly and gain control of a rally.

Base Position

A back-row player needs to be able to move quickly and react decisively to dig balls. Stand in a ready position that allows those movements, as compact and low to the ground as possible (figure 6.1). In general, it is more beneficial to stay square to the attacker. Your weight is on the balls of your feet with your right foot in front of the left. Your knees and waist are bent so that when you look down, your knees are over your toes and your shoulders are over your knees. Your arms are bent at the elbows and your palms face the opponent with your thumbs pointed back. This compact position allows you to move quickly to the ball and also allows you to extend your platform and play the ball if it is attacked directly at you.

Figure 6.1 **BASE POSITION FOR THE DIG**

1. Stand low to the ground.
2. Square to the attacker.
3. Stand with weight on balls of feet and right foot in front of left, feet hip-width apart.
4. Bend knees and waist.
5. Bend elbows.
6. Face palms toward opponent with thumbs back.

MISSTEP

You square to the target.

CORRECTION

A good defender faces the source of the ball (the server or the attacker) and then adjusts his or her platform to direct the ball to the target. When you square to the target first, it reduces the chance of a quality contact.

Footwork

Defensive footwork serves two main purposes. The first is to provide a preparatory move into the correct defensive position; the second is to pursue the ball. When moving from one defensive position to another, take quick, short steps so that you can easily stop on balance when the ball is attacked. This is one of the most critical elements of playing defense

Even when the ball is attacked right at your position, footwork is required. Move your feet from hip-width apart and your right foot forward to being wide. Your feet need to be firmly planted when you are digging balls that are attacked directly at your body. When digging, it is difficult to make up for an imbalance; imbalances usually show in the uncontrollability of the dig.

The step-hop (figure 6.2), which is the basic footwork for passing, is also the basic footwork pattern for defense. Start in a low, defensive ready position. Take a step in the direction of the path of the ball with the foot closest to where the ball will land. Take a quick hop, jumping more laterally than up and down, so that you land on both feet with your right foot slightly in front of the left and your base wide.

Figure 6.2   STEP-HOP DEFENSIVE FOOTWORK

1. Begin in a low defensive stance.
2. Step in the direction of the ball's path with foot closest to where the ball will land.
3. Take a quick hop.
4. Land on both feet with right foot slightly in front of left, base wide.

Often you will have to break into a sprint to run down a ball that is perfectly placed or deflected off the block. When this happens, start with short strides and extend into longer ones as you accelerate to chase the ball. Try to stay as low as possible as you run so that you don't have to adjust too much when you finally arrive at the ball.

Platform Presentation

Always extend your arms to meet the ball as far away from the body as possible. Your goal is for the ball to make solid contact on your forearms (figure 6.3a). As with passing, it is up to the digger to manipulate her footwork and platform presentation to contact the ball in a position that will send it to the target area.

When you are unable to use footwork to get your body all the way to the ball, you will have to reach outside of your body line and dig the ball nonlinearly. Extend your arms to the ball, align your thumbs by placing one palm in the other, and drop the shoulder that is closest to your target area to get your platform behind the path of the ball (figure 6.3b).

Figure 6.3 **CONTACTING THE BALL**

Linear Contact

1. Extend arms to meet ball.
2. Contact ball on forearms.
3. Direct ball to target area, minimizing arm swing.

Nonlinear Contact

1. Extend arms to the ball, reaching outside body line.
2. Align thumbs by placing one palm in the other.
3. Drop shoulder closest to target area.
4. Contact ball on forearms.
5. Direct ball to target area, minimizing arm swing.

Because of the velocity of an attacked ball, the margin for error is much greater than on a served ball. The main difference between digging and passing is that the target area for a dig is much larger and farther off the net (figure 6.4). It is more important to make sure that your team gets the opportunity at a swing than to make a perfect pass and run your full offense. One way to make sure you don't dig the ball too tight to the net is to bend the elbows at contact to redirect the ball up (figure 6.5).

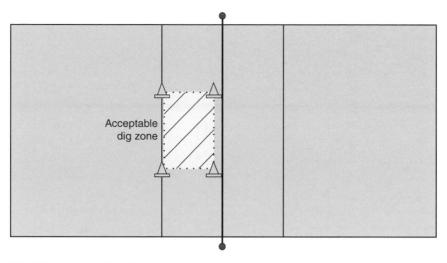

Figure 6.4 Target area for the dig.

Figure 6.5 Bend elbows at contact to redirect ball up.

MISSTEP

You swing the arms to dig.

CORRECTION

Hold your shoulders tight so that the action is more of a rebound than a pass. Too much movement from the arms results in the ball ricocheting wildly off the platform.

Diving and Rolling

Anyone who says volleyball is not a contact sport hasn't seen a libero diving around the court to keep the ball off the floor. While most volleyball players wear knee pads, they are not necessary if you dive using proper technique. The key to diving is to start in a low position and maintain it through the movement. To dive safely and make effective contact on the ball, follow these steps. Take a step with the foot closest to the ball while maintaining a low body position (figure 6.6a). Pushing off the planted foot, extend your leg as you reach for the ball with your platform (figure 6.6b). Turn your knee in so that it exposes the hip you will land on (figure 6.6c). If you can't get two arms on the ball, then reach out with the arm that allows you to keep your torso facing the net. Keep your chin up throughout the dive in order to avoid contact with the floor.

Remember that things can happen very quickly in a rally and you must get back on your feet quickly. Because you will end up on your side after diving for a ball, it is easy to keep your momentum going and roll over your back to get your feet under you (figure 6.6d). Some players also swing their bottom leg over their shoulder to roll back into position, while others roll onto their chest and do a push-up. Regardless of how you get ready for the next contact, you should react quickly and be prepared.

Figure 6.6   **DIVING AND ROLLING**

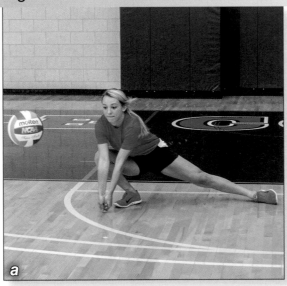

Preparation

1. Maintain low body position.
2. Step with foot closest to ball.

Dive

1. Push off planted foot and extend leg.
2. Reach for ball.
3. Make contact with platform.

Follow-Through

1. Turn knee in to open hip.
2. Keep chin up.
3. Land on hip.

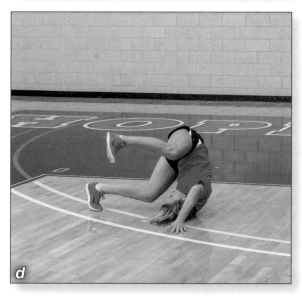

Roll

1. Roll over to back.
2. Position feet under you.
3. Stand up.
4. Return to defensive ready position.

MISSTEP

Many players simply fall in their effort to go for a ball.

CORRECTION

Make sure that the leg you stepped with is fully extended after you dive for the ball. Extending your leg can help you get to balls 2 or 3 feet (.6-1 m) farther away.

Collapse Digging

A particularly challenging ball to defend is the one attacked directly in front of you at your feet because it is difficult to get as low as you need to and stay squared to the attacker. For this type of situation, collapse by bending your knees in and to the ground. (Wear knee pads if you use this technique.) At the same time, extend your platform but bend your elbows so that you are able to get your forearms under the ball (figure 6.7). You will finish the dig on your knees and with your forearms on the floor. The ball should be headed high in the air back in the direction it came from.

Figure 6.7 COLLAPSE DIG

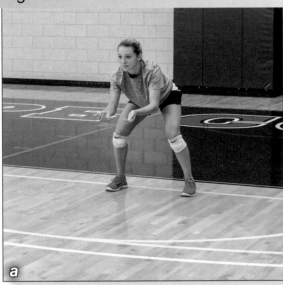

Preparation

1. Ball is attacked directly in front of you at your feet.
2. Bend knees in and to the ground.
3. Extend platform but bend elbows.

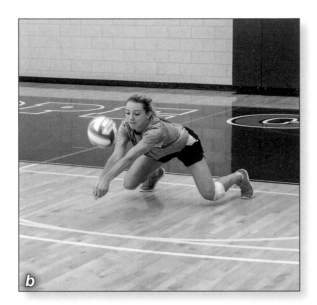

Execution

1. Position forearms under ball.
2. Make contact.

Follow-Through

1. Finish dig on knees, with forearms on floor.
2. Hit ball high in the air.
3. Extend forward through the ball.

Overhead Digging

When you are in a shallow defensive position and the ball is attacked deep in the court, use the overhead digging technique (figure 6.8) to keep the ball in play. Staying square to the attacker, move into position to contact the ball within your shoulders. Set your weight on your back foot. Because when passing, your hands are not as strong as your platform, the weight transfer from your back foot to your front foot (left to right) is critical. Bring your hands up to your head with your thumbs back just as you would in overhead passing. The major difference between overhead passing and digging is in how stiff to make your wrists. A ball attacked softly can be passed with the same overhead passing technique discussed in step 2. When the ball is attacked harder, stiffen the wrists with the palms facing the back of the ball. Focus contact on the heel of the hand with the palms and fingers contacting afterward in an effort to direct the ball up. The harder the ball is attacked, the stiffer your hands should be on contact, otherwise you will not provide enough resistive force to redirect the ball to your teammates.

Figure 6.8 **OVERHEAD DIG**

Preparation

1. Stay square to attacker.
2. Move to contact ball within shoulders.
3. Put weight on back foot.

Execution

1. Lift hands to head with thumbs back.
2. Stiffen the hands, palms facing ball.
3. Contact the ball on the heels of the hands.
4. Contact the ball with palms and fingers after contacting with heels.
5. Direct ball up.

Pursuit

You have the most control over a ball when you are stopped, on balance, and able to transfer weight through the ball. However, sometimes you are not able to get to the ball fast enough that you can stop and achieve balance. Tipped balls, block deflections, or balls pushed to the corners require you to run through the ball as you play it with your forearms. Keeping your shoulders low, run to the ball and extend your platform so that you make contact under the ball. By continuing to run through the ball, your horizontal momentum will transfer into the upward trajectory of the pass and you will maintain consistent balance throughout the play.

MISSTEP
You try to perfectly pass the ball to the middle of the court when chasing after it.

CORRECTION
If you have two contacts left, you only need to pop the ball straight up. Your teammates should be following you and will be close enough to line up a free ball to the other side. Trying to play the ball all the way back to the middle of the court requires a strong contact that if executed poorly will make the ball more difficult to play.

Digging Technique Drill 1   **Partner Digging**

Stand with a partner on the same side of the net. Have your partner attack a ball to you specifically to work on linear and nonlinear forearm digging, overhead digging, and forward movement to cover the tip. The attacker should catch the dig in order to allow the defender to recover and ensure a quality toss and consistent hand contact. Perform 10 digs and then switch responsibilities.

TO INCREASE DIFFICULTY
- Your partner attacks to locations farther away from you to expand your range.
- Your partner attacks with greater pace and force to simulate a harder-attacked ball.
- The attacker doesn't tell the digger where he plans to attack.

TO DECREASE DIFFICULTY
- The attacker keeps attacks close to the digger's position.
- The attacker uses a slower arm swing.
- The attacker tells the digger where he plans to attack.

Success Check
- Extend arms completely.
- Contact behind and below the path of the incoming ball.
- Direct the ball to the target area, minimizing arm swing.

Score Your Success
Earn 1 point for each successful dig (10 attempts).
Your score ___

Digging Technique Drill 2   **Diving Progression**

Diving for a ball can be scary at first. This partner progression will make it less painful. Knee pads are helpful, but not necessary. Another training tool is wearing a sock over your hand in order to prevent floor burns.

Step 1: Start with your left knee on the ground and right knee at a 45-degree angle. Face your partner with the ball. As the ball is tossed, extend your platform and turn your knee in so that you roll and contact the outside of your leg and hip with the ground. Contact the ball with both arms of your platform. To advance the drill, the attacker tosses the ball farther so the digger can extend only one arm. Try five times and switch roles with your partner.

Step 2: Start on two staggered feet with your hips low and right foot forward, as if you had already taken a step. Bend your right knee to lower yourself as close to the ground as possible. As the ball is tossed, extend your platform and turn your knee in so that you roll and contact the ground with the outside of your leg and hip. Contact the ball on both arms of your platform. To advance the drill, the attacker tosses the ball farther so the digger can extend only one arm. Try this progression five times in each direction and switch roles with your partner.

Step 3: Start in a ready position and take a step with your right foot. Bend your right knee to lower yourself as close to the ground as possible. As the ball is tossed, extend your platform and turn your knee in so that you roll and contact the ground on the outside of your leg and hip. Contact the ball with both arms of your platform. To advance the drill, the attacker tosses the ball farther so the digger can extend only one arm. Try this progression five times in both directions.

Progress from a toss to a throw to a roll shot and then a hard-driven attack.

TO INCREASE DIFFICULTY

- The attacker attacks to locations farther away from the digger to expand range.
- The attacker attacks with greater pace and force to simulate a harder-attacked ball.
- The attacker doesn't tell the digger where she plans to attack.

TO DECREASE DIFFICULTY

- The attacker keeps attacks closer to the digger's position.
- The attacker uses a slower arm swing.
- The attacker tells the digger where she plans to attack.

Success Check

- Start as low to the ground as you comfortably can.
- Try to play as many of the balls as you can with your platform (rather than a one-hand extension).
- Turn your knee so that the hip takes the brunt of the fall.

Score Your Success

Step 1: Earn 1 point for each successful dig (5 attempts).

Step 2: Earn 1 point for each successful dig (5 attempts).

Step 3: Earn 1 point for each successful dig (5 attempts).

Your score ____

Digging Technique Drill 3 **Run-Throughs**

Divide players into groups with an odd number of players in each group. Players form a single-file line in the back corner of the court. An instructor stands in the opposite corner of the court near the net and tosses balls alternately along the sideline and end line and forces the players to run through the ball (figure 6.9). After digging, the player returns to the back of the line and goes along the opposite line for a second repetition. Each player digs 10 balls and then the group switches to the other back corner of the court to perform the drill from a different angle.

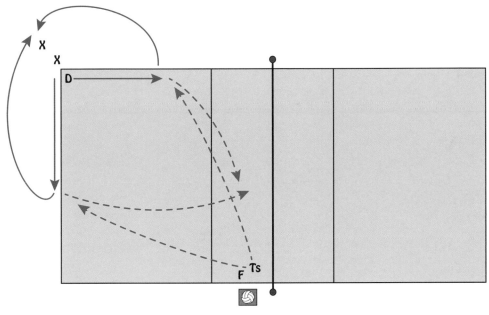

Figure 6.9 Run-throughs.

TO INCREASE DIFFICULTY

- Require a certain number of passes without an overpass.
- Lead the digger farther so that she has to cover more ground.
- Attack balls that are faster and lower.

TO DECREASE DIFFICULTY

- Add loft to the toss to the passer.
- Keep the pace of the drill slow.
- Toss the ball closer to the digger.

Success Check

- Stay low as you run through the ball.
- Position your platform under the ball.
- Keep the pass off the net.

Score Your Success

Earn 1 point for each successful dig (10 attempts).

Your score ___

Digging Technique Drill 4 **Digging the Arc**

The objective of this drill is to develop the ability to accurately dig balls attacked laterally. An attacker stands at the net in the middle of the court and faces a single digger on the end line. The attacker should attack the ball to the digger's left as the digger steps to the left and plays the ball outside his or her body line. The digger recovers and repeats in the same direction until he or she gets to the sideline (figure 6.10). The attacker then hits to the digger's right until he or she returns to the end line, continuing to advance to the right-back sideline. Take turns as the attacker and digger.

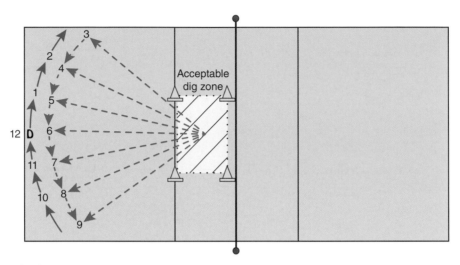

Figure 6.10   Digging the arc.

TO INCREASE DIFFICULTY

- The attacker attacks with more pace.
- The attacker makes the digger cover more distance with each hit.

TO DECREASE DIFFICULTY

- The attacker slows his arm swing to hit easier balls to dig.
- The attacker aims the attack just outside the defender's body line.

Success Check

- Stay low.
- Step in the direction of the ball.
- Drop the shoulder to get behind the ball's path.

Score Your Success

Earn 1 point for each successful dig (10 attempts).

Your score ___

Digging Technique Drill 5   **Up and Down Digging**

The objective of this drill is to get comfortable diving and playing multiple types of attacked balls. An attacker stands at the net on the same side of the court as a digger in middle back. The attacker hits a ball at the digger that requires her to dive. The digger should get up and get set to dig another ball immediately attacked in similar fashion. When the digger gets too close to the attacker, balls should be tossed to the deep corner and the digger executes a run-through. If the digger doesn't need to dive to play the ball, she must still drop down to the floor and get up after each ball.

TO INCREASE DIFFICULTY

- The attacker increases the speed of the drill by attacking the next ball faster.
- The attacker expands the digger's range by attacking farther away from the digger.
- The attacker increases the pace of the attack by hitting harder.
- The target area is made smaller.

TO DECREASE DIFFICULTY

- The attacker decreases the speed of the drill by attacking the next ball slower.
- The attacker limits the digger's range by attacking closer to the digger.
- The attacker decreases the pace of the attack by hitting with a slower arm swing.
- The target area is made larger.

Success Check

- Read the attacker's arm swing to predict where she will attack.
- Maintain a stationary, balanced position at hitter's contact.
- Give all-out effort even for balls that you believe to be out of reach.

Score Your Success

Earn 1 point for each successful dig (15 attempts).

Your score ___

DIGGING TACTICS

Being a good digger means having solid technique but also an acute awareness of what is happening on the court and what may happen. The art of reading hitters is developed through practice and game experience.

Reading Hitters

Some defenders look impressive because they dive around the court making spectacular saves. The best defenders, however, seldom have to dive because they can predict where the ball will go and put themselves in a balanced position to play the ball with control. These diggers are skilled at reading the opponent's offense and an entire book could be written about that skill alone. For the beginning volleyball player, here are a few things to watch that will help you read the hitter and predict where she will attack.

ANGLE OF APPROACH

Most volleyball hitters tend to hit in the direction that they approach. If their approach is angled sharp to the set, then they will attack sharp crosscourt. If their approach starts inside the court and goes toward the sidelines, they will tend to attack the line. Identify the hitter's starting position and put yourself on the same extended line of where they are approaching.

SET LOCATION IN RELATIONSHIP TO THE BLOCK

The block creates a shadow of space on the court to which it is impossible for a hard-driven ball to be attacked. When you find yourself in that space, move to an area that can be attacked or commit to covering the tip over the block.

PLANT IN RELATIONSHIP TO THE BALL

Many hitters give away where they are going to attack by how they plant to the ball. For instance, if a hitter jumps to attack and the set falls short of her body, then she will almost always have to attack crosscourt. Likewise if she plants too far inside, then the only shot open is the line.

ELBOW

Hitters with powerful arm swings use a high elbow to contact the ball hard and fast, but in order to tip a ball, contact must be made below the ball to avoid the block. Watching the hitter's elbow is an important cue for predicting her intentions. If you see a hitter's elbow drop and her hand move under the ball, then it is likely she will tip the ball shallow in the court.

TENDENCIES

While thinking about the tendencies of a hitter isn't necessarily reading what is happening on the opponent's court, you should keep a mental note of what opposing hitters have tried before. If it was successful, they might continue to exploit the strategy until you make an adjustment. Sometimes hitters have only one shot in their arsenal.

The challenge with novice volleyball players is that because of inconsistent technique and hand contact, they are sometimes harder to read than advanced players. The best advice is to put yourself in a position that keeps the court in front of you and to remain stationary at contact so that you can react to wherever the ball goes.

MISSTEP

You move into position while the ball is being contacted.

CORRECTION

Be stationary at contact even if you are sure you know where the ball will go. A last-second redirection with the wrist, a mishit, or block deflection could cause the ball to react differently than you predicted. To then stop, change direction, and pursue the ball will almost always make you late to playing it.

Digging Target

As we established earlier, you want to dig a ball to a different location than where you pass a ball in serve receive or off a free ball. A higher dig is better than a lower dig, a ball dug off the net is better than a ball dug too tight, and a dig to the middle of the court is better than a dig to the sidelines. A perfect dig is one that is passed 15 to 20 feet (4.6-6.1 m) in the air, 7 to 12 feet (2.1-3.6 m) off the net, and near the middle of the court. To dig with consistency, keep the following considerations in mind.

LINE DIGGING

When you are digging along the sideline, square up to the hitter with your feet and hips, and drop your inside shoulder so that the ball will redirect to the middle of the court (figure 6.11). Because you usually will be responsible for digging the hard-driven ball and the tip, you should be in a position that allows you to easily move forward as well as get your hands up to dig overhead.

Figure 6.11 When digging along the sideline, square to the hitter with your feet and hips and drop your inside shoulder.

SEAM DIGGING

When you are positioned in the middle back, square to your hitter and drop your inside shoulder (when the attack is coming from the pin), but to a much lesser degree. It is important for the seam digger to keep a narrow base because of the necessity to pursue balls that deflect off the block or are attacked to the deep corners.

CROSSCOURT DIGGING

The crosscourt digger is generally both squared to the hitter and target area, but that doesn't mean his job is easier. Make sure you get all the way to your line to keep the court in front of you and be ready to use the collapse digging technique to play balls that are attacked in front of your feet.

OFF-BLOCKER DIGGING

As an off-blocker, you are primarily responsible for defending two specific shots. One is the off-speed ball played to the middle of the court that you will play with your forearms. The other shot is the sharp crosscourt attack that you will play with the overhead digging technique. Regardless of which shot you play, the most important adjustment you need to make is giving enough height to the dig that you have time to complete the skill and transition out to your hitting position. This will also ensure that despite the shallow attack, the other hitters in the front row will also be able to transition effectively.

MISSTEP

You do not get high enough on your line in defensive positioning.

CORRECTION

By putting yourself on your line about 12 feet (3.6 m) from the net, even if you have to make poor contact with the ball, you have teammates close enough to pursue the ball. When you are too deep and make a poor contact, the ball will usually ricochet in a direction where no one else is in position to play it.

Parallels

The most vulnerable place in any defense is the seam between two players' responsibilities. When a ball is attacked into this seam, the player who is closer to the net will, generally, take the ball hit shallow and the player farther away should play the ball hit deeper. Both players should go for the ball because movement will be required before they know exactly whose ball it is. Understanding their responsibilities will help them know which balls to play.

Playing the Deep and Tipped Balls

The never-ending struggle in defensive positioning is how to play the hard-driven deep ball and cover the tip. Proficiency in the overhead digging technique allows you to take a more shallow defensive position that will reduce the distance you will have to move to cover the tip. Make sure that your weight is always on the balls of your feet and that at contact you are stationary and have a narrow base in order to react and move to where the ball is played.

Digging Tactics Drill 1 **Reading the Game**

Watching video can help to slow the game so that specific cues can be observed for processing. Find footage from a match online and pause the action between contacts. Use the information you gather as you look around the court and predict what will happen next. Where is the server likely to serve based on the alignment of her hips? Where will the setter set given her hand contact location? What positions on the court can the hitter attack given the location of the set in relationship to the block? Evaluate 10 specific contacts and predict the result. Keep track of your accuracy.

TO INCREASE DIFFICULTY

- Pause the action earlier before contact to limit the amount of available information.
- Pause and look away from the screen so that you have to rely on what you remember seeing.

TO DECREASE DIFFICULTY

- Pause the action closer to the event that you are trying to predict.
- Look for clues on the defensive side of the ball to see what they are reading.

Success Check

- Watch the angle of momentum.
- Watch how players square to specific directions.
- Focus on the relationship between body positioning and the location of the ball.

Score Your Success

Earn 1 point for every correct prediction (10 attempts).

Your score ___

Digging Tactics Drill 2   **Repetition Digging**

The objective of this drill is to drop the appropriate shoulder to dig to target while staying squared to alternating hitters. This drill involves three diggers in left back (LB), middle back (MB), and right back (RB) and two attackers standing at the net, or on boxes, across the net in the left front (LF) and right front (RF). Attackers should hit in the following sequence so that every position digs from each hitter.

1. LF attacks down the line to the RB
2. RF attacks seam to the MB
3. LF attacks crosscourt to the LB
4. RF attacks crosscourt to the RB
5. LF attacks seam to the MB
6. RF attacks line to the LB

Go through three cycles and switch defenders.

TO INCREASE DIFFICULTY

- The attacker attacks to locations farther away from the digger to expand range.
- The attacker attacks with greater pace to simulate a harder-attacked ball.
- Mix in tipped balls or blocking deflections.

TO DECREASE DIFFICULTY

- The attacker keeps attacks closer to the digger's position.
- The attacker uses a slower arm swing.
- Make the target location smaller and require a higher dig.

Success Check

- Stay low with weight forward.
- Remain stationary at contact.
- Play under the ball with two hands.
- Count any ball that is played up and into the court.

Score Your Success

Dig to the acceptable dig zone = 2 points

Dig anywhere in the court = 1 point

Your score ___

Digging Tactics Drill 3 **Tip, Dig, Overhead**

This drill teaches players how to defend three types of balls. An attacker can be anywhere along the net and the digger can be in any back-row position. Three balls in a row are attacked at the digger: a tip, a hard-driven ball to the digger, and a hard-driven ball requiring an overhead dig. The balls can come in any order, and the digger must remain in a neutral ready position to defend them. Go through the cycle of attacking (tip, forearms, overhead) three times for a total of nine balls plus one bonus ball of any variety.

TO INCREASE DIFFICULTY

- The attacker attacks with greater pace to shorten the digger's decision-making time.
- The attacker should try to fake one type of attack and force the digger to react.

TO DECREASE DIFFICULTY

- The attacker goes slowly, allowing more preparation time.
- The attacker tells the defender what type of attack is coming.

Success Check

- Square to the source of the ball.
- Position platform under the attacked ball.
- Keep elbows in and hands high to enable quick reactions.

Score Your Success

Earn 1 point for each dig to the acceptable dig zone.

Your score ___

SUCCESS SUMMARY

Learning to dig requires discipline, effort, and fearlessness. By staying low and reacting quickly to get your platform to the ball, you will save a lot of points and set up your team's success. Remember to read your opponent's approach and arm swing as well as where your teammates are playing defense, to put yourself in a better position to make the dig. When you have achieved at least 65 points on the drills and feel confident in your ability to dig with accuracy, you can take the next step toward understanding team offense.

Digging Technique Drills

1. Partner digging   ___ out of 10
2. Diving progression   ___ out of 15
3. Run-throughs   ___ out of 10
4. Digging the arc   ___ out of 10
5. Up and down digging   ___ out of 15

Digging Tactics Drills

1. Reading the game   ___ out of 10
2. Repetition digging   ___ out of 12
3. Tip, dig, overhead   ___ out of 10
   Total   ___ **out of 92**

Team Offense

The modern volleyball offense is designed in much the same way as a football team executing a strong running game: by using multiple set tempos and the entire length of the net, the setter finds a hole in the opponent's block for the hitter to attack. While you might not be there yet, this strategy is effective at every level and makes watching the game played at high levels that much more exciting. This step describes offensive systems, the varieties of sets possible, how those sets can be used in combination with each other to create holes in the defense, and what players need to consider when designing an offensive strategy.

OFFENSIVE SYSTEMS

Offenses are set up by identifying specific roles for the players on the court. In some situations, such as family reunions and pickup games in the sand, role specialization is not important. As competitive level increases, role specialization can be the difference between winning or losing every point of the match. Specialization can happen in both the front row and back row because of the special considerations in playing each position. Keep in mind that players must maintain rotational order until the ball is served. After that, players rotate into base positions, their specialized spots in the front or back row. The descriptions in this section advance from simple to complicated. The first number refers to the number of hitters on the court and the second number is the number of setters.

MISSTEP

Designing an offense around someone other than the setter.

CORRECTION

Even if you have one dominant athlete as a hitter, you should always focus on the setter first. Ideally, the setter is involved in every rally and has the opportunity to influence not just her own contact but the third as well.

6-6

The 6-6 (figure 7.1) is the most basic offense and can barely be called a system. In the 6-6 there are six hitters and six setters. Optimally, one setter is designated by the position on the court she is playing. For instance, whenever a player rotates into the middle front, she is the setter for that rotation. Everyone gets the opportunity to hit and set in this system, which is recommended for novice players, pickup games, and youth teams below age 12.

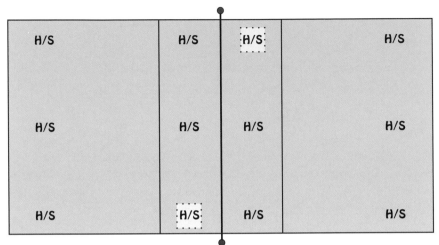

The player who rotates into the square is the setter for that rotation.

Figure 7.1 6-6 offensive system.

When choosing the location of the designated setter, consider the effectiveness of the back set. If the backset is too difficult, then designating the setter position as the right front would be advantageous because the setter can set two hitters instead of one. If your team has at least one person who has playing experience or demonstrates strong ball-control skills, consider running an offense that allows that athlete to specialize in a setting role.

4-2

The 4-2 (figure 7.2) consists of four hitters and two setters, who are lined up opposite each other on the court. When the designated setters rotate into the front row, they play their base position in the middle or right front, depending on their ability to back set. The other two front-row players can specialize in playing left front and middle or right front.

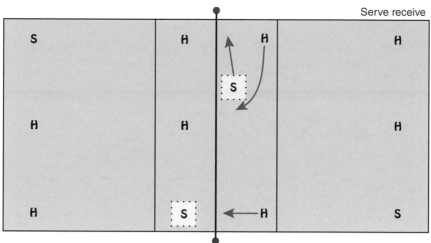

Front-row setter is the designated setter in each rotation.

Figure 7.2 4-2 offensive system.

The advantages of the 4-2 over the 6-6 include more consistency in setting and the opportunity to specialize at the hitting positions. However, the 4-2 reduces the learning opportunities of playing every position on the court, which is a disadvantage, especially for youth players.

6-2

The 6-2 (figure 7.3) offers six hitters and two setters, with three front-row hitters at all times. In this offensive system, two designated setting positions in the rotation hit when they are in the front row and set from the back row. The base position for the setter in the back row is in the right back because it is the closest to the target passing area just to the right of center at the net.

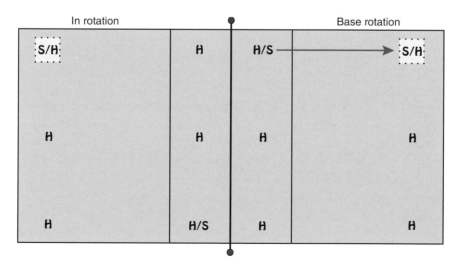

Figure 7.3 6-2 offensive system.

The most significant advantage of the 6-2 is that it keeps three hitters in the front row, but it can also provide flexibility in defensive specialization. If a setter is not a very good blocker, the 6-2 can be a way to bring in a formidable block on the right side for the rotations during which he or she is in the front row. The 6-2 has seen a resurgence in popularity at the highest levels of competition, but it has one significant drawback. Different setters bring a different rhythm to the game and it can be difficult for hitters to adjust to even subtle setting differences.

5-1

The most common offensive system is the 5-1 (figure 7.4) with five hitters and one setter who sets in both the front and back rows. Despite the disadvantage of having only two hitters in the front row for three rotations, teams are able to run the slide attack or put greater emphasis on the back-row attack. The other advantage of having a front-row setter is her ability to attack the second contact. Having an athletic setter who is capable of playing the ball high above the net doesn't just provide the opportunity to run a fast offense. The setter can also be an offensive threat with the dump that poses problems for the block and in turn opens up opportunities for other hitters.

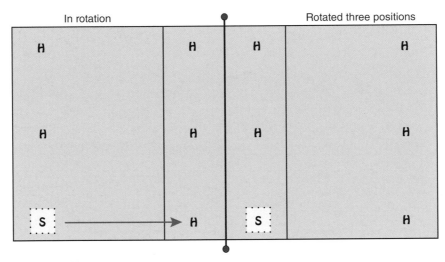

Figure 7.4 5-1 offensive system.

ATTACKING VARIATIONS

A variable-tempo offense is one in which the setter uses a variety of set heights and distances to prevent a solid double block from the opponent. The best way to do this is by running an offense that forces a blocker to move and jump (commit) with a hitter because of the speed of the set. Ideally, all of the sets across the front row would be that fast, but as the set speed increases, so does the likelihood of error. The compromise is to set three different tempos to three different hitters at different places along the net. There is always a quick option (first tempo), a seam attack (second tempo), and a release (third tempo) set if something goes wrong. We will discuss how these sets are used in combination with each other later, but first let's discuss each set.

Every team has a different way to name a set, and communication is important for ensuring the hitters and setters know what to do. Some use names, letters, or hand signals to identify each set. For our purposes, we will use a system of two-digit numbers in which the first number represents the meter-long zone of the net the hitter attacks from (from left to right), and the second number indicates the set tempo (first, second, or third). For consistency, we will identify the ideal setting location as being the sixth meter along the net.

First Tempo

While the setter dump is the fastest attack that an offense can run, the first-tempo set is a close second. The first tempo is a set with an extremely flat trajectory and in some situations makes a straight line from the setter's hands to the hitter's reach. This attack requires the hitter to approach as the pass is arriving at the setter. Ideally, the hitter is in the air with his arm cocked and ready to swing while the setter is contacting the ball. The setter then pushes the ball to the hitter's reach in a straight line. Table 7.1 lists the three first-tempo sets for you to practice.

Table 7.1 First-Tempo Sets

Set name	Description	Key for the setter	Key for the hitter
31	This set is attacked in the third meter inside from the left antenna by either the left-side hitter or the middle. To time this appropriately, the hitter should leave the ground as the pass enters the setter's hands.	Push the ball flat on the set so that if the hitter were to miss it, it would keep going to the left side. The left side should be ready to pass the ball over in this situation.	Square up to the setter even if your approach takes you away from her. Attacking the right back will exploit the seam between the middle and right-side blockers.
51	This set is attacked in the middle of the court and is the easiest of the first-tempo sets to execute. The hitter should be in the air as the setter contacts the ball.	Jump setting can make the tempo of this set even faster and requires the ball to be in the air for less time, which reduces the margin of error.	Don't get too tight to the net. You need room to swing around the block.
71	This set is attacked immediately behind the setter by a middle hitter running a slide or a right side using a two-footed approach. The set is similar to the 51, but behind the setter instead of in front.	If your hitter is right-handed, you will put the ball on the right side of the zone. If left-handed, you can set the ball in the middle of the zone.	When using the slide approach, jump from a position in line with the setter and fly to the ball. Planting your foot behind the setter will force you to overrun the set and limit your attacks.

First-tempo sets are challenging because they require trust and consistency between the setter and hitter. But they are critical in forcing an opponent's middle blocker to commit to this hitter.

MISSTEP

Setting the quick set with too much arc.

CORRECTION

Keep the tempo fast in order to get the opponent's middle to commit.

Second Tempo

The second-tempo set is used in combination with the first to force a seam in the block. If the first tempo is fast enough and the middle has to commit in order to get at least one blocker stopping that hitter, the second tempo is just fast enough to make it difficult for the blocker to recover and get to that hitter. In the trajectory of second-tempo sets, the peak of the arc is never higher than the top of the antenna and can be attacked at any place along the net. Table 7.2 lists four common second-tempo sets.

Table 7.2   Second-Tempo Sets

Set name	Description	Key for the setter	Key for the hitter
12	All the way to the left pin, this set will be difficult for a middle to close even without a first-tempo decoy. The hitter should jump immediately after the ball is set.	Keep this set off the net, especially when you are setting from anywhere off the net, but make sure you continue to transfer your weight forward.	Attack the seam that will almost assuredly be there between the pin blocker and the late-arriving middle. Keep a high elbow in order to adjust to subtle inconsistencies in set distance.
32	This set is in the third meter and is an inside set that gives the left-side hitter different angles to hit around the block. The hitter should jump immediately after the ball is set.	Because you don't need to worry about setting all the way to the pin, bring your contact point farther back on your head to fake a back set.	Try not to give away this set too early by shuffling all the way into the court immediately. Wait from your normal position and approach aggressively to the ball using a four-step approach.
52	The second-tempo set in the middle of the court should be run only when a first-tempo set is well established. It is primarily set to the left- and right-side hitters.	Keep this set off the net in case the block is able to recover and all three are up. Use this set in serve receive when a pin hitter is at the opposite antenna as a way to get her closer to her base.	As with the 32, do not give away this set too early. Wait as long as you can and approach as fast as you can to minimize the time blockers have to set up.
92	This is a faster back set that travels to the right antenna and can be attacked by either the right side off two feet or the middle off one foot. Both hitters should jump immediately after the ball is set.	Make sure that you square up to the left antenna in order to make the opponent's middle think you are setting there. The set must go all the way to the right antenna to make the line shot an option.	Attack the line in order to beat both the block getting all the way out to the pin as well as the left back who will be late getting to her line.

The back-row attack also is used regularly as a second-tempo option because it can be used even when a team is passing poorly. If the setter is pulled off the net 10 to 15 feet (3-4.6 m), a gentle lob set that doesn't go very high can be an effective offensive option in a difficult situation. When the back-row hitter gets set, she should be aware of the opponent's base blocking positions to try to attack through the seams at the net.

Third Tempo

The third tempo is a release set for when a setter is out of position. Third-tempo sets are higher than the antenna and follow a trajectory that produces very little horizontal movement of the ball when the hitter makes contact. This allows the hitter to know exactly where she needs to plant in order to attack with maximal reach. These sets are usually set to the pin attackers to avoid a triple block in front of the hitter if the set were made to the middle (although that sometimes occurs at the pins as well). This set should be farther inside the court and off the net than other sets in order to give the hitter room to work around the block. Sometimes referred to as a 5 × 5 ball (because it is ideally 5 feet [1.5 m] off the net and 5 feet inside the court), a setter should set this ball only in desperation. To successfully attack this set, hitters should plant tight to the ball to maximize reach, and contact low on the ball to avoid the strongest part of the block. The goal on this attack is not to get a kill, but to prevent the opponent from getting a pass that allows them to set all three hitters. The last thing a hitter should do in this situation is take an aggressive risk that might result in attacking the ball out of bounds or into the net.

MISSTEP
Pushing the third-tempo set too tight or close to the pin.

CORRECTION
Give your hitter time and space to attack by making the set high, inside, and off the net.

IN-SYSTEM OFFENSE

When your team makes a pass that gives the setter multiple options, the likelihood of scoring a point significantly increases. What tactics can you employ to maximize your chances?

Two Hitters

When the setter is front row and you have two hitters, you need either the opponent's middle to jump with your middle or move in a direction opposite your second tempo hitter. Table 7.3 lists options.

Table 7.3   Offensive Options With a Front-Row Setter

Left side	Middle	Setter	Tactic
12	51	Dump	If you can establish the setter as an offensive threat and run the 51 fast enough, every attacker will have a solo block.
52	31	Dump	The 31 will draw the opponent middle to the 31, and their right-side blocker will run into the middle, leaving a seam in the middle of the court. The opponent's left side should step up to block, but you might catch him watching.
32	92	Dump	The combination of offensive setter and slide attack is one of the most difficult to defend. Because of the communication involved, blockers get confused about who they are supposed to block and either the setter or the slide hitter is usually left with no one blocking! The 12 to the left side will almost always have a split in the block if the 12 is set fast enough.

Three Hitters

When you have a back-row setter, the combination plays that you can run are exciting. Table 7.4 lists a few.

Table 7.4   Offensive Options With a Back-Row Setter

Left side	Middle	Right side	Tactic
12	51	92	When running a 51 with the middle, you will spread out the pin sets as much as possible. The intent is to force the middle blocker to jump with the 51. If you were to set a 32 or 52 with either pin hitter, the middle might have time to recover and double block the second tempo.
52	31	92	A crossing play between the middle hitter and left side will force the opponent's blockers to communicate who is taking what. With all the action on the left side of the court, it also opens up a seam for the right side to hit the 92.
32	71	52	Running the middle on a quick-slide 71 behind the setter will tempt both the opponent's left-side blocker and middle blocker to commit. That would leave no blocker against the right-side attack at either the antenna or in the middle. The left-side would be left with a solo blocker.
12	92	71	You can also run a crossing play behind the setter in which the right side goes in for a 71 off two feet and the middle runs a slide to the pin in the 92.

OUT-OF-SYSTEM OFFENSE

Passing isn't always perfect. In fact, more often than not, you will find yourself and your team out of system, in which your setter and hitters are adapting to an imperfect pass. At times, the pass will be so bad that the only hope for the setter is to throw it up in a third-tempo set to a pin (5 × 5 set), but most of the time the setter will be somewhere between being in and out of system. The following are ways your team can still be in system when the pass is just OK.

Connecting With the Middle

When the pass is right on the net, the middle goes right to the setter to run a 51. When the pass is off the net, the hitter takes an approach angled 45 degrees and attacks the ball at the same distance away from the setter as he or she is off the net. For instance, if the pass pulls the setter 8 feet (2.4 m) off the net, the middle approaches to a spot 8 feet away from the setter at a 45-degree angle. Obviously, no one is bringing out a tape measure. The point is that the 51 is not set to a spot but rather is a relationship. The farther the pass is off the net, the farther the attacker approaches from the setter. The tempo remains as fast as possible, but remember that the ball has to cover distance and it would be impossible to run it at the same speed.

MISSTEP

When the middle keeps her feet and hips closed to the setter when pulled out of system.

CORRECTION

Getting away from the setter allows you to open up your feet and hips to the set. This allows the ball to pass through a much wider hitting window.

Reversing the Flow

Volleyball has a rhythm and a flow to it. Sometimes when the pass is not good, the only way to try to create solo blocking situations for a hitter is to reverse the flow. If the pass brings you forward, set backward; if the pass brings you backward, push it out front. Opposing blockers and diggers tend to shadow the setter and move in similar directions. By reversing the flow you keep them off guard.

Knowing How to Err

The most important job of the setter is to set hittable balls, but not necessarily perfect ones. Knowing how to err is important, especially when the pass is not perfect and the setter has to make adjustments. Even when not perfect, the set should still give the hitter time and space. Being too far out, too tight, too low, or too fast limits the hitter's options. Erring on the side of being too far in, too off, too high, and too slow still gives the hitter a chance to take a full swing.

Using the Back-Row Attack

Don't forget about the hitters in the back row and don't let them forget that they can be a viable option, especially out of system. The back-row attack is difficult to block because the hitter is so far away from the net. That means that the hitter can swing aggressively with less risk than a front-row player.

Using the Setter Dump

Sometimes your team will be out of system because the set is too tight to the net and all the setter can do is try to save it. The alternative is to take advantage of the tight pass and attack on the second contact. The setter dump can also be effective when the setter is off the net because not many defenses expect it. If the setter has a reputation for setting the middle even when he or she is off the net, a quick middle set and one that extends farther across the net look similar to a defensive player in the back row. This can be used to your advantage in less-than-ideal situations.

COVERAGE

Having your back-row players come shallow behind a hitter as coverage in case of a blocked attack really belongs in the chapter on team defense. Because it happens at the same time as the attack, we will discuss it here. Proper coverage allows the hitter to swing aggressively and risk being blocked. This is advantageous because most blocks are not well established and tooling the block can be a very successful strategy.

Getting into a coverage posture (figure 7.5) is easy. You want to be as low to the ground as possible to give yourself maximum time to react to the blocked ball. Your hands should be out, with your palms up so that if you need to make a quick lunge for the ball, you can with one hand. Your eyes should be up and already looking at the blocker's hands before the ball is contacted. This visual cue allows you to communicate instructions to the hitter about whether she should hit line, angle, or seam. It also helps you because you might not be able to watch the attack and react to the ricochet off the block fast enough. The change of direction is quick and can be difficult to follow, so focus your attention on where the ball will go after it hits the blocker's hands.

Figure 7.5 **COVERAGE POSITION**

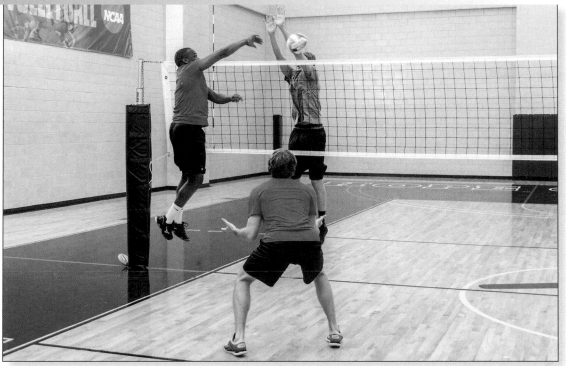

1. Low to the ground.
2. Hands out, palms up.
3. Eyes up and looking at blocker's hands.

While coverage posture might be easy, coverage positions can be complicated. These three guidelines should make this simple and effective:

1. The closest back-row player to the hitter is the *primary* coverage. For the right-side hitter, the primary coverage would be the right back. The primary-coverage person should take a position on the court side of the pin attacker or directly behind a middle attacker.

2. The back-row player farthest from the hitter is the *deep* coverage. Sometimes a ball can be attacked off the block and it travels all the way back to the end line.

3. Everyone else should be square up to the hitter and in a low position, ready to make a play.

After you are in the correct position, if you are able to cover a blocked ball, be sure to pass it high and to the middle of the court. A high pass will ensure that all players can shift from coverage positions to attacking positions.

MISSTEP

Covering the right side attacker when the setter is back row presents a specific challenge. In most situations the right back would have primary coverage responsibilities. When that player is the setter, they are out of position to be directly behind the attacker. Primary coverage for the right side when the setter is back row.

CORRECTION

In this situation, the middle back would become the primary coverage player moving directly behind the hitter along the right sideline. The left back would sink deep in the court to cover balls along the endline.

OFFENSIVE CONSIDERATIONS

Having an offense in place and hitters who know where to go is only half the battle. As you continue to step forward in this game, you will learn to take advantage of every opportunity your opponent gives you and how the tactical decisions you make can sometimes cost more points than they earn. As with many skills in this sport, striking the balance between risk and reward is critical to long-term success.

Matchups

Before every play, the entire team should be looking for the blocking matchups that might give your team an advantage. Maybe after your team rotates you realize that a player 10 inches (2.5 cm) shorter than you is lined up to block. You want to signal your setter so that your team can exploit the obvious matchup opportunity. This works in the opposite direction as well. If you have a strong hitter matched up against a good blocker, you might run a play that moves the hitter away from the defensive strength. For instance, if I notice that a great blocker rotates into the front row to play left side and my best hitter is a right side, I would call a play that sends the right side in for a 52 to avoid the disadvantageous matchup. Pay attention to what is happening on the other side of the net because each rotation presents a different matchup that can be exploited.

MISSTEP

Making assumptions about your skills, or those of your opponent, based on height. For example, short players are not necessarily poor blockers.

CORRECTION

Use experience, scouting, or statistics to learn where vulnerabilities are in the opponent's defense.

Tempo vs. Success

Making your offense as quick as possible might create seams in the block and prevent the defense from getting set, but it also offers trade-offs. A quick offense limits the options that hitters can take advantage of and sometimes results in poor contacts by the hitters. Increasing the speed of your team's offense without reducing its effectiveness is a balancing act. There is nothing wrong with putting a little more loft on a set to facilitate a hitter's effectiveness. Remember, however, that making one player more effective might reduce the effectiveness of another. If you have a middle hitter who is struggling to make good contact with a 51, you might want to slow down. However, a slower first-tempo set means that the middle blocker does not need to commit. In this situation, a double block is all but guaranteed for every other hitter in the front row.

Proper Judgment

Never attempt anything tactically that you cannot do technically. Just because it is ideal to run a variable-tempo offense doesn't mean you should. The challenge in managing a team is flirting with the line between skill and challenge. If your team lacks athleticism, skill, or understanding of the game, then you should keep it simple. However, most teams find their flow when they are pushed a little outside their comfort zone.

Team Offensive Drill 1   +5 With Full Front Row

Set up three hitters and a setter on side A and six defenders on side B, and have the setter on side A designate three play sets (combinations of attacks to run off a free ball). Just before the instructor tosses a ball to the setter, he or she should call out the play set so that the front row knows what they are running. The offensive team attempts to kill that ball against the defense and, if they do, they get a point. If the defense keeps the ball alive but is not able to aggressively counterattack (defined as any play involving a jump and full arm swing), then no point is scored (wash). If the defense is able to block the attack or dig well enough to get an aggressive counterattack, a point is subtracted from the attacking team's score. Scoring only one side is called tug-of-war scoring. The defense wins if the offense's score is negative 5, and the offense wins when they get to positive 5 points. Everyone should change offensive and defensive and positional roles and start again, but everyone gets two opportunities to be on offense in two different roles (setter and outside hitter, outside hitter and middle, middle and setter).

TO INCREASE DIFFICULTY

- Increase the number of offensive plays that the offensive team can run.
- Tell offensive players to use deception in their attacking and not to hit where they are facing.
- Start each rally with a dig from a coach's attack to force out-of-system adjustments.

(continued)

Team Offensive Drill 1 *(continued)*

TO DECREASE DIFFICULTY

- Limit the number of offensive options for the offense (only one hitter can score points, no setter dumps are allowed, and so on).
- Tell attackers to hit where they face.
- Have the toss keep the setter in-system for every ball.

Success Check

- Know your responsibility in every offensive play.
- Hitters should look for advantageous vulnerabilities in the defense.
- Setters should look for advantageous matchups.

Score Your Success

Offensive team wins = 5 points for offensive players

Defensive team wins = 2 points for offensive players

Your score ___

Team Offensive Drill 2   **Hot Seat**

How do you get kills when the defense knows that you are getting the ball? The hot-seat drill challenges one hitter to find ways to win rallies because she is the only hitter allowed to score points for her team. This will challenge you to work around a solid double block. Start each rally with the instructor tossing a ball into the defense on alternating sides of the court. One designated hitter for both teams is allowed to score points. Errors do not result in points for either team. Each game is played to 10 points and then teams switch personnel and responsibilities. Everyone should be in the hot seat once.

TO INCREASE DIFFICULTY

- Start each rally with a down ball into the defense instead of a toss.
- Increase the variety of sets that the hot seat hitter is able to attack.

TO DECREASE DIFFICULTY

- An easy toss to the defense starts every rally in system.
- Limit the types of sets the hot-seat hitter can receive.

Success Check

- Focus on efficient transition footwork from offense to defense.
- Never attack to the same location twice in a row.
- Use off-speed attacks to keep the defense off-balance.

- The defense should focus on getting their blockers and diggers set to defend the hot-seat hitter over other players.

Score Your Success

The hot-seat hitter is awarded the number of points he or she earned.

Your score ___

Team Offensive Drill 3   **Continuous Coverage**

Assign six players to one side of the net in base positions. Toss in a free ball from the other side and have them pass, set, and attack. At the same time that they are attacking, toss another ball over the attacker to simulate the attack being blocked to test the coverage positions. Continue until a ball is attacked into the net, a ball lands on the court, or the players seem too tired to continue. This is a great drill for developing out-of-system skills. Perform drill for one minute and keep track of how many balls in a row are successfully covered and attacked over the net. After one minute, change positions and play again.

TO INCREASE DIFFICULTY

- Have the defense focus on transitioning and attacking faster tempo sets or combination plays instead of high outside sets.
- Challenge the coverage with balls that are more difficult to cover (through into the seams, open areas, or in front of hitters to force them to cover their own attack).

TO DECREASE DIFFICULTY

- Toss balls in for coverage that are slow and have loft.
- Focus on keeping balls in play by encouraging roll shots from the defense that are low risk.

Success Check

- Stay low in coverage.
- Balance the court.
- Watch the block (tossed ball), not the hitter.
- Pass the covered ball high to give your hitters time to transition.

Score Your Success

6 or more balls in a row covered and attacked = 10 points

3 to 5 balls in a row covered and attacked = 6 points

Fewer than 3 balls in a row covered and attacked = 2 points

Your score ___

Team Offensive Drill 4
BRAWFRO (Back-Row Attack With Front-Row Option)

This drill uses three back-row players, a front-row setter, and a front-row hitter on both sides of the net. Free balls are initiated to alternating sides, and the game is played to a certain number of kills (with hitting errors counting as negative points). Back-row attack kills are worth two points. Use the following matchups:

- Left side vs. left side with setters blocking (option 1, figure 7.6*a*).
- Middle vs. middle (option 2, figure 7.6*b*).
- Left side vs. right side with the setter in the right back (option 3, figure 7.6*c*).
- Middle vs. middle.
- Right side vs. left side with the setter in the right back.

Play to 10 points, with the winning team winning by 2 points.

TO INCREASE DIFFICULTY

- Begin the rally with a down ball instead of a free ball.
- Increase the variety of sets that the hot-seat hitter is able to attack.

TO DECREASE DIFFICULTY

- Use an easy toss to the defense to start every rally in system.
- Limit the types of sets the hot-seat hitter can receive.

Success Check

- Plant to the ball to give yourself multiple offensive options.
- Try to attack the ball off the block if the ball is set too tightly.
- Use off-speed hits and deception to keep the defense off-balance.
- Attack at the setter to prevent her from running an offense.

Score Your Success

The winning team earns 10 points. The other teams earns the number of points they received during the drill, not to exceed 10 points.

Your score ___

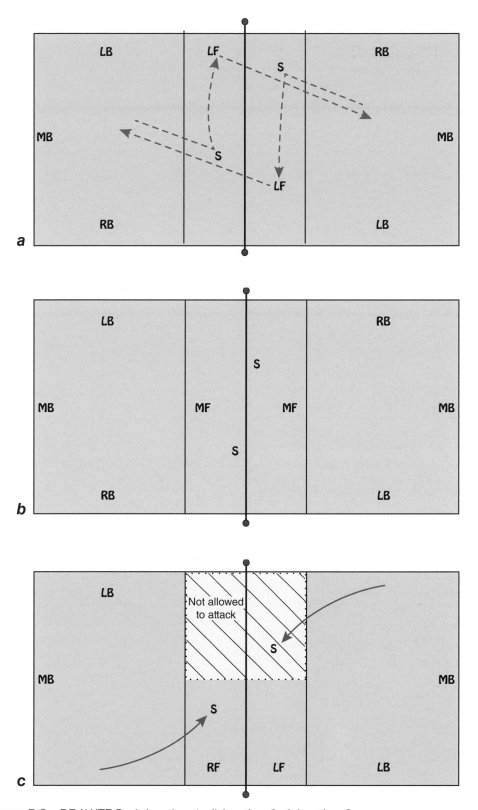

Figure 7.6 BRAWFRO: *(a)* option 1, *(b)* option 2, *(c)* option 3.

SUCCESS SUMMARY

Putting the offensive puzzle together requires communication and focus. It requires every player to focus on what is happening on both sides of the net and to analyze the team's strengths and weaknesses in each rotation. As you attend to the advantages in your matchups and the tempo that gives your team the most consistent chance for success, know that there is always a way to win a volleyball rally. After you have demonstrated your offensive proficiency by earning at least 25 points in the drills and feel confident in your ability to run an offense that is deliberate and consistent, you can take the next step to understanding team defense.

Team Offensive Drills

1.	+5 with full front row	___out of 10
2.	Hot seat	___out of 10
3.	Continuous coverage	___out of 10
4.	BRAWFRO (back-row attack with front-row option)	___out of 10
	Total	**___out of 40**

Team Defense

Three fundamental rules apply to playing team defense in volleyball:

1. It's everyone's ball.
2. Don't let the ball touch the floor without maximal effort.
3. The reward of discipline is trust.

The first rule is an answer to the question, "Whose ball was that?" It is common when discussing team defense to allocate court-area responsibilities based on position (for instance, the right back is responsible for the line attack). While there are important distinctions to be made, in the end, keeping the ball off the floor is everyone's responsibility.

The second rule addresses aggressiveness and effort in your defense. A maximal effort is one in which you dive for a ball even if it is out of your reach, where you sprint after a ball that is heading to the bathrooms. You never know what you are capable of getting to and you might surprise yourself. Even if you don't get it, your teammates and your opponent will respect the effort.

By being disciplined in knowing the areas of the court you are primarily responsible for in the defense, as the third rule suggests, you will allow others to be disciplined as well. When you abandon a specific responsibility (for instance, defending the setter dump) you might cause another player to be out of position as she makes up for your carelessness. When you are disciplined and do your job, it creates a feeling of trust on the court that also results in effective team play.

As you step forward in your understanding of volleyball, you will master the man-back (perimeter), rotation, man-up (rover), and middle-middle defenses as well as understand option blocking and how to effectively use the libero.

MAN-BACK (PERIMETER) DEFENSE

The basic concept behind the man-back defense is that it is easier to play balls that are attacked in front of you than behind you. This defense also gives players the freedom to read the game because they are seldom limited to playing only one ball (tip coverage, for instance). It is the most flexible defense for making tactical blocking and defensive adjustments. The base positions of this defense find the front row players in either a bunch block or spread formation and the back row in an inverted narrow triangle (figure 8.1). The wing defenders (LB and RB) are primarily responsible for covering the setter dump, and the middle back for patrolling the back line for balls sent deep.

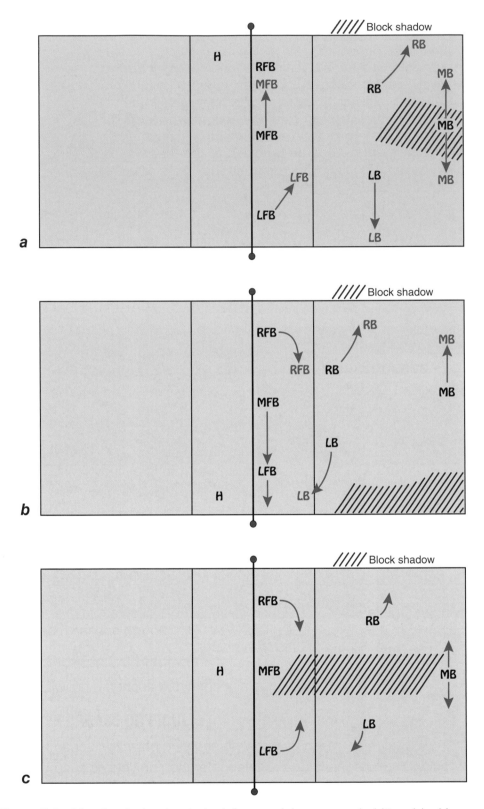

Figure 8.1 Man-back (perimeter) defense: *(a)* versus pin-hitter blocking angle, *(b)* versus pin-hitter blocking line, and *(c)* versus middle hitter.

DEFENDING PIN ATTACKERS

- Blockers: Blockers can take either line or angle.
- Line digger: When the block takes line, the line digger should move shallow to cover the tip. When the block takes angle, the line digger should place his outside foot on the sideline and play as deep as he can and still run forward to cover a tip over the block.
- Seam digger: The middle back reads the distance of the set in relation to the block. If the set is pushed past the block but inside the antenna, the middle back should move toward the line 3 to 5 feet (1-1.5 m). If the set falls short of the block, the middle back reads to the left to dig the deep crosscourt attack. If the ball falls behind a closed block, the middle back holds the middle position and prepares to pursue a ball attacked high and over the block or off the blocker's hands. When there is a seam in the block, the middle back will take a few steps forward to be ready to cover the middle of the court.
- Crosscourt digger: The crosscourt digger moves from the base position in the court to the sideline as the ball is set. The digger's outside foot is on the sideline 13 to 15 feet (4-4.6 m) from the net, with the hips squared to the attacker. It is important for the digger to get to this position quickly so that the digger, from this location, can read the hitter and move to where he or she thinks the ball will be attacked. Do not give up the sideline position until you are sure the attacker cannot attack it because of his or her arm swing or plant placement.
- Off-blocker: If the block is taking the line, the off-blocker is less responsible for tips (covered by the line digger) and more responsible for the sharp crosscourt attack. The off-blocker should step off the net about 9 feet (2.7 m) (just inside the 10-foot [3 m] line) and approximately 5 feet (1.5 m) in from the sideline. If the block is taking angle, the off-blocker should step in 10 feet (3 m) from the sideline and approximately 7 feet (2.1 m) from the net. This gives the off-blocker the opportunity to dig the sharp crosscourt shot as well as cover tips into the middle of the court.

MISSTEP

You read without getting to the sideline.

CORRECTION

By getting to the sideline first, you defend the spot on the court that is easiest to attack as well as position yourself to get to more balls.

DEFENDING THE MIDDLE ATTACK

- Blockers: It is the middle blocker's job to stay with the opponent's middle wherever she goes. If your team is bunch blocking, the right-side blocker can help with the 31 and the left-side blocker can help with the 51 and 71. When the opponent's setter is in the front row, the left-side blocker should be fronting the setter and should be a step away from helping with the middle.

- Left-back digger: The ideal position for the wing defenders (left and right back) against an attack from the middle is 15 feet (4.6 m) deep on the sidelines. When the left front helps on the block, the left back comes up the sideline to cover tips because the sideline is in the block's shadow. Defending a quick middle in perimeter defense is a challenge because it is difficult to get to the sidelines and stopped fast enough.

- Right-back digger: The right back gets out to the sideline from base position to cover the setter dump. Make sure that you are stopped at contact and squared back to the middle in order to make a quality dig. If the left-front blocker is helping and the left back has moved up the line to cover the tip, you can move deeper (18 feet [5.5 m] from the net) in order to cover the deep cut back to zone 1.

- Middle-back digger: The middle back watches how the block lines up against the set, just like when defending the pins. If the ball gets out past the block, the digger should move in that direction along the end line.

- Off-blocker: If a pin is unable to help on the block, she should take one quick step off the net, square to the hitter, and be ready to cover the tip. When you do play the ball, make sure you pull it off the net and give it height to ensure a quality set and swing.

MISSTEP

You are still moving out to the sideline during or after contact.

CORRECTION

A good defender sacrifices being in the right place for being stationary at contact. Even if you can't get all the way to your defensive position, make sure you are stopped so that you can make a play on the ball without having to change direction.

ROTATION DEFENSE

Rotation defense (figure 8.2) gives specific responsibilities to each player. Often it is used by teams who want to commit their defensive players to specific locations so that they do not need to make reading decisions. Rotation defense can also be used when your opponent shows specific tendencies.

The crux of rotation defense involves blocking angle at the antennas, committing the wing defender on the line side to the tip while the middle back rotates to the line. The crosscourt digger and off-blocker cover the crosscourt with the left back reading into the seam in the block (if there is one). It is important to have quick players in the crosscourt digging positions when playing a rotation defense because of the amount of court they are asked to cover. Base positions to cover the setter dump and defense against a middle attack are the same as in perimeter defense.

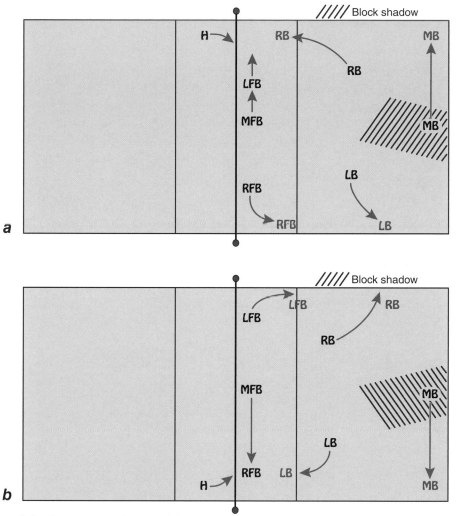

Figure 8.2 Rotation defense: *(a)* versus left-side attacker and *(b)* versus right-side attacker.

DEFENDING PIN ATTACKERS

- Blockers: Take the deep angle (essentially zone 6) away from the hitter by lining up the pin blocker's outside hand on the attacker's swinging arm.

- Line digger: The wing defender on the attacker's side steps forward from his base position until he is behind the block and covering the tip. He should be in position to cover the tip to the middle of the court just over the block but also able reach the sideline or the net on a dive.

- Seam digger: The middle-back digger is responsible for covering the line attack at both antennae. As the set is pushed to the pin, the middle back follows the set all the way to the line. The middle back still has reading to do within the 10 feet (3 m) of the end line that the block is not covering. A hitter with strong ball control can attack a ball back toward the middle of the court when the set is pushed far enough to the antenna and the blocker doesn't adjust. While her primary responsibility is the ball attacked right down the line, she continues to use her reading skills to know when to stay inside.

- Crosscourt digger: The crosscourt digger has a lot of court to cover and should move from the base position inside, covering the setter dump, to the sideline about 17 feet (5.2 m) deep. This allows the crosscourt digger to take a deep crosscourt position and puts her in position to chase after a ball attacked into zone 6 over the block.
- Off-blocker: The off-blocker steps directly off the net to the 10-foot (3 m) line or slightly beyond in order to dig the sharp crosscourt attack.

MISSTEP

You cover an area of the court that the antenna won't let a hitter attack.

CORRECTION

When the ball is set past the antenna, it is impossible for the hitter to attack the line. The middle back should move his or her defensive position to the crosscourt.

MAN-UP (ROVER) DEFENSE

One of the drawbacks of both perimeter and rotation defenses is that the base positions to cover the setter dump sometimes require the diggers to move in the opposite direction of where the set is going. This movement often results in players still moving at the point of contact or being late to make the appropriate read. One solution to this problem is to flip the triangle of base positions to put two players in the back corners of the court and one player near the 10-foot (3 m) line in the middle and covering the setter dump (figure 8.3).

In this defense, the two primary diggers in the backcourt are able to constantly read the play because they have to move only laterally or forward. This defense is advantageous because it reduces the amount of movement to cover both the setter dump and the attackers. Because it is used less often, it can be difficult for offenses to adjust to when they are used to attacking areas on the court vulnerable in perimeter defense. In general, blockers will bunch block in order to protect the middle back.

DEFENDING PIN ATTACKERS

- Blockers: The most important aspect of blocking pin attackers in the rover defense is to take away their ability to attack to middle back. Middles should be proficient at closing the block. The pin blocker should line up her outside hand on the hitter's arm swing.
- Line digger: Similar to playing the middle back in a rotation defense, the line digger reads the distance of the set in relation to the block, the hitter's approach pattern, and the arm swing to determine where to be at the hitter's contact. The range is a span about 10 feet (3 m) wide. The line digger must keep the court in front of her.

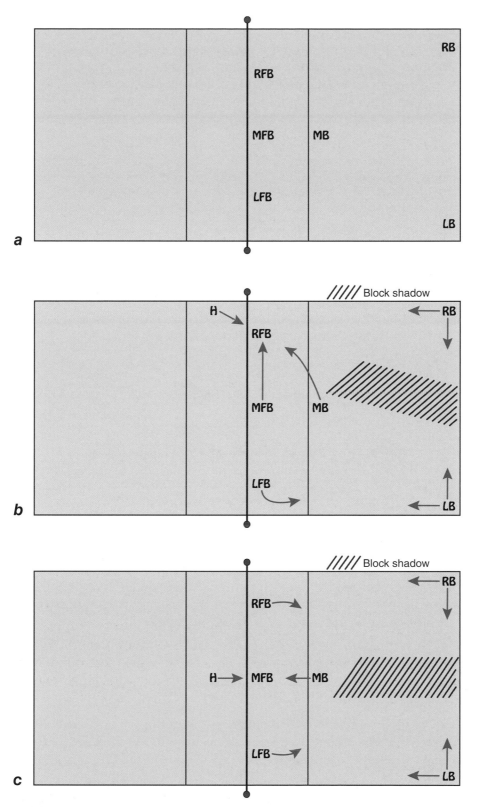

Figure 8.3 Man-up defense: *(a)* base positions, *(b)* versus pin attacker, and *(c)* versus middle attacker.

- Rover: The player at the top of the triangle is called the rover because she covers the tip across the entire net. Because of her importance in defending the setter dump, it is important that the rover mirror the setter's movement. If the setter gets pulled forward or pushed back, then the rover moves with her. Once the ball is set to a pin, the rover takes a defensive position on the inside of the 10-foot (3 m) line that is a dive away from the sideline and the middle of the net.

- Crosscourt digger: The crosscourt digger reads the distance of the set, the hitter's approach, and the hitter's arm swing to defend the entire deep crosscourt. If the ball is on the inside of either the block or the hitter, then the crosscourt digger should read a sharper shot and find a position higher on the sideline. If the set is outside of the block or hitter, defending deeper is advised.

- Off-blocker: The off-blocker defends the sharp crosscourt shot and should move to a position near the 10-foot (3 m) line and 2 to 3 feet (.6-1 m) in from the sideline. When a ball is attacked into the seam between the off-blocker and crosscourt digger, the off-blocker plays the short ball and the crosscourt digger plays the deep ball.

MISSTEP

You run a rover defense with middles who are unable to close the block.

CORRECTION

When the middles are struggling to close the block, it is time to run a different defense or get in the gym to improve this skill. A seam in the block makes the backcourt extremely vulnerable.

Note: You can defend a seam in the block in two ways. The easiest is for the crosscourt digger to come into the court 5 feet (1.5 m) and read the hitter through the seam. This allows the rover to play the tip or the block deflection. This does expose more of the court to a sharp crosscourt shot, although some of that is taken up with the late middle blocker. If you are worried about the sharp crosscourt attack, you may want your crosscourt digger to continue defending it and let your rover sink deeper to defend zone 6 with an overhead dig.

DEFENDING THE MIDDLE ATTACK

- Blockers: Blockers should always line up in order to take away the middle of the court. When the opponent is in system, the middle blocker should commit to blocking the opponent's middle hitter. No matter where the middle hitter attacks from, the middle blocker must stay with the middle hitter and jump with her. The middle blocker should also try to contact as many balls as possible with her hands even if it means reaching outside her body line and reducing how far she can reach over the net. This is advised in the rover defense only because of the increased number of defenders in position to cover the tip and block deflection. A block deflection is more likely to be covered in this defense and the risk is worth the reward.

- Rover: The rover aligns himself directly behind the block at the 10-foot (3 m) line. When there is a double block on the middle, the rover should shift to the side where the double block is coming from in order to balance the tip coverage responsibilities with the off-blocker and cover more area of the court.

- Line and crosscourt diggers: It is helpful for the wing defenders in the back row to know the hitting tendencies of the opponent. Some middles are able to attack sharp angles (attacking to the sidelines 12 to 15 feet [3.6-4.6 m] deep, whereas others attack exclusively to the deep corners. Knowing the hitter's tendency will determine how far you come up to play defense. The safest place to start is on the setter's release to a middle hitter; try to get to a position on the sideline about 20 feet (6.1 m) from the net. Remain stationary at hitter's contact. Even if you find yourself in the shadow of the block, do not move farther up the line. Many balls are played high over or off the blocker's hands, and moving too far up the sideline takes you out of position to defend those balls.

- Off-blockers: If a pin blocker cannot help on the block, she should quickly step off the net and get into a low defensive ready position to help cover the block deflection or tip. The rover will split the difference between the sideline from where the block is coming from and the off-blocker.

MISSTEP

In a rover defense, a blocker reads the hitter's arm swing to take away a specific angle from the hitter.

CORRECTION

Focus on simply defending the middle back with your block and don't jump into either the power angle or cut back because you think the attacker is going to hit there. Quick middle attacks are difficult to read and by guessing, you will expose too much open court behind you.

MIDDLE-MIDDLE DEFENSE

The middle-middle defense is based on the idea that a majority of the balls attacked in volleyball land in or pass through the middle of the court. In this defense, you place your best digger in the middle of the court (15 feet [4.6 m] from the net and 15 feet from both sidelines) and encourage him to touch as many balls as possible by any means necessary (figure 8.4). The wing defenders take positions 2 feet (.6 m) beyond the 10-foot (3 m) line and 2 feet (.6 m) in from the sidelines. Blockers can be in either a bunch or spread system, depending on the threat from the middle hitter or the quality of his technique.

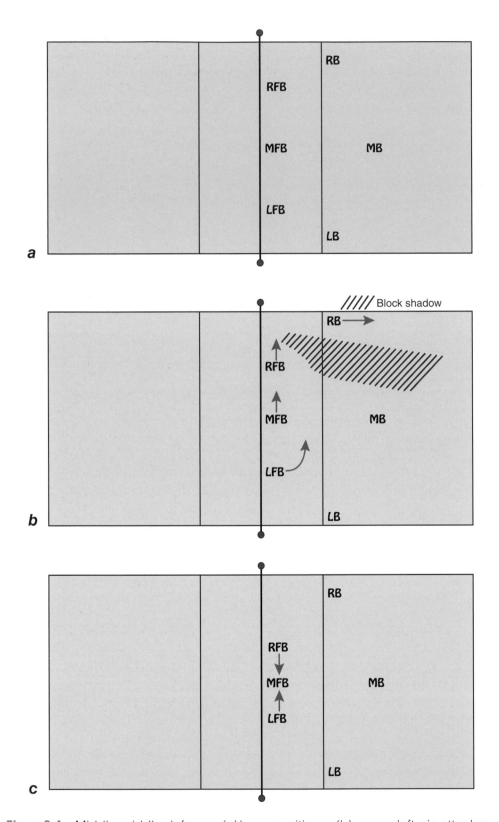

Figure 8.4 Middle-middle defense: *(a)* base positions, *(b)* versus left-pin attacker, and *(c)* versus middle attack.

Like the rover defense, there is little movement from base positions covering the setter dump to the defensive read positions. This reduces the frequency of players being out of position and of moving at the point of contact. One of the major advantages of this defense is that it is intuitive. If you asked three novice volleyball players to start playing defense in the back row without any instruction, most would line up three shallow players in a straight line across the back row. It is also a reactionary defense, meaning that the diggers do very little reading, if any. They already are in positions where, statistically, the greatest number of balls land. You do not need to have a high volleyball IQ to play this defense well, but you should have players who are quick and relentlessly try to get to the ball. The disadvantage of this defense is that it exposes striking vulnerabilities that take training to reduce.

DEFENDING PIN ATTACKERS

- Blockers: The most vulnerable spot on the court when playing a middle-middle defense against a pin hitter is the seam between zones 1 and 6 in the backcourt. This is a relatively easy shot for the hitter and comes at an awkward angle for both the middle-middle and the line digger to make the play. It is important that the blockers take this area of the court away at both antennae by aligning the middle of the pin blocker's body with the hitter's arm swing.

- Line digger: The line digger moves backward into a flat position aligned with the middle-middle, approximately 3 feet (1 m) from where he started. This digger is responsible for the line attack as well as deflected balls that come off the block out of bounds. The line digger uses the overhead digging technique to play any hard-driven ball attacked through an 8-foot (2.4 m) lane on the line side of the court.

- Middle-middle: The middle-middle is usually a strong digger whose job is to make contact with the majority of balls. As the ball gets set to the antenna, the middle-middle simply turns his feet and hips to square up to the attacker. He should always wait until the ball is contacted and see where it is going before moving anywhere else. A good defensive principle is to have your best defender dig the most balls. If you know where the most balls will either land or pass through the middle of the court, then that is where your best digger should be. This is also a good position for a taller player who is not as quick to dive to the floor but has strong ball control skills and quick reflexes. In general, the position of the middle-middle is 15 feet (4.6 m) from the net and 15 feet from the sidelines, although positioning depth is somewhat affected by height. It is important for the middle-middle to play a lot of balls with the overhead digging technique. Shorter players may not be able to play some hard-driven balls that would land deep in the court at the 15-foot (4.6 m) depth. In this situation, you may want to move the digger back to a depth at which she can cover the back line. The middle-middle tries to play as many balls as possible, but will defer to the crosscourt digger on balls attacked deep to the crosscourt sideline. This defender should be ready, however, to chase down a ball attacked high and deep down the line because it usually will be over the head of the line digger. To train for both these ball situations, an instructor should conduct a drill that focuses on the first-step pursuit required in this defense. This drill is similar to the run-through drill from step 6, except that the digger starts in the middle of the court and pursues to the corners.

- Crosscourt digger: Like the line digger, the crosscourt digger starts 2 feet (.6 m) in from the sideline and 2 feet farther deep from the 10-foot (3 m) line. The only movement the crosscourt digger makes is to square up to the attacker. Just like the middle-middle, she should not move from her position 2 feet in and 2 feet off until she can see exactly where the ball is being attacked. The crosscourt digger may have to use the overhead dig to play balls attacked into the deep corner, but she mainly will use the forearm dig.

- Off-blocker: The off-blocker is responsible for covering tips in the middle-middle defense and should take a position 5 feet (1.5 m) from the net and halfway between the sidelines. This may seem like a long way to go, but the off-blocker is the player to cover the tip right over the block along the sideline. It is also important that the off-blocker come that far into the court in order to stay out of the crosscourt digger's line when defending crosscourt attacks.

MISSTEP

You make extraneous movement before contact.

CORRECTION

Stay still and be patient before pursuing the ball. Middle-middle defense is sometimes most difficult for experienced players to learn because they have been taught their whole life to move around the court before contact and to get into a ready position. This usually puts players out of position in this defense and prevents them from being able to make a quick reaction to play the ball.

DEFENDING THE MIDDLE ATTACK

- Blockers: As with many other defenses, it is to your advantage to get a double block, rather than a solo block, on a middle hitter. Even when it is not possible, try to get two blockers to the ball and align the block to take away the corner closest to the hitter. For instance, when a middle hitter attacks a 31, the block will want to take away the right-back corner from the hitter. This will expose more area for the middle-middle digger.

- Back-row diggers: All back-row diggers stay in their base defensive positions until the ball is attacked and they can clearly see where it is going.

- Off-blocker: The off-blocker should step off the net and into the court to prepare for a tipped ball. Even if the off-blocker cannot get into that position in time, she should be stationary at contact and in a low, defensive ready position to react and play the ball if it is attacked in her direction.

OPTION BLOCKING

The importance of blocking grows as the level of play goes up. At the highest levels, blocking is incredibly important, while at the youth and recreational levels its influence is significantly less (there are many other aspects of the game to worry about). One strategy for improving the effectiveness of a block is to adjust your base positions around a blocking tactic, called option blocking.

Let's say your team is serving and your best blocker is also your left-side hitter. The opponent's best hitter is also their left side and they have been hitting over your smaller right-side player. In option blocking, you exchange your best blocker (even though she usually plays on the left side) with the right side to get a better blocking matchup against your opponent's best hitter. Because you are serving, you have to play defense before having the opportunity to go on offense, so making sure you have the best defensive front possible is a higher priority. You should think about how you will make the transition out of this when you get the chance to swing. Will the left side stay on the right side or will you try to get her back to her most comfortable attacking position?

Another option-blocking strategy is to make an early commitment to a specific hitter. For instance, if the left-side hitter has been particularly effective and your middle has been late closing the block, you may want the middle to go to the left side even before the ball is set. If the opponent's setter does not recognize what you are doing, she will set her hitter into a strong double block. If she does recognize what you are doing, then she might set a different hitter who, even against a solo block, might not be as effective.

Option blocking is effective only when you have versatile players who can make adjustments quickly. It can be incredibly fun to watch two high-level teams start making adjustments with their defenses and blocks to find an advantage or counter an opponent's adjustment.

EFFECTIVELY USING THE LIBERO

As was discussed earlier in The Sport of Volleyball section, the libero is a position that was added to the game in 1998 to lengthen rallies and reduce the advantage seen by offenses. The libero does not follow normal subbing rules, which allows your best defender to stay in the backcourt the majority of the time. The following are ways to ensure your team uses this position to its full potential.

Make sure the libero is a good passer. Defense should not be the only aspect that you think about when determining the libero. In fact, while the intent behind creating the libero position was to increase the effectiveness of the defense, volleyball saw an improvement in the offense because of increased serve-receive quality. Shift your serve-receive pattern so that the libero is in the middle of the pattern and you will greatly improve the likelihood of an in-system pass off serve.

Channel the attack to your libero. Use the block to entice your opponent to attack your libero. Even if it is the opponent's best shot, do not block the area of the court that your best digger is defending.

Put your libero in a position with the greatest defensive responsibility. Assuming that the strength of most opponents is attacking from the left side and you are running either a rotation or rover defense, your libero should be in the left back. If you are running a middle-middle defense, then the libero should generally be in the middle-middle position. When playing a perimeter defense, look at the skills of the player when determining whether he should be in middle back or left back because both positions hold significant responsibility. Of course, there are always exceptions to these guidelines, so if you go against them, carefully consider the rationale.

When the setter makes the first contact, whose responsibility is it to set the ball? It used to be common for the setter, after taking the first contact, to pass the ball to the right side for the set. Now it is more common for the setter to dig to the middle of the court where the libero can set to either the right or left side. Remember that the libero can use her hands to set only if she is behind the 10-foot (3 m) line. As more emphasis is placed on a strong right-side attack, having the libero take the second ball creates a solid out-of-system attacking option.

Don't be afraid to think creatively in your use of the libero. Just because the vast majority of liberos play left back doesn't mean they have to, and just because the vast majority of liberos play defense for the middles doesn't mean that they have to. Think creatively not just to use all of the talents of the player you have in that position, but to deceive the opponent as well. Maybe your libero is incredible at covering blocked balls, but because she is playing in the middle back of a perimeter defense, she is not the primary coverage for the majority of your hitters. Moving the libero into the left back and changing your defensive system might be warranted. Maybe you have a middle hitter who is better at defending than your left side. Using your libero effectively might mean having her play three rotations for a middle and two rotations for a left side. Understand the rules of the position, but don't be limited by conventional strategies.

MISSTEP

The libero commits setting violations.

CORRECTION

Remember that the libero cannot overhead set to an attacker in front of the 10-foot (3 m) line. To avoid confusion, the libero should become accurate at forearm passing to a hitter for the attack. Also, remember that if the libero defends a tipped ball with her hands in front of the 10-foot line, the front-row setter is not allowed to attack it above the plane of the net.

TEAM DEFENSIVE DRILLS

These drills are 6v6 scrimmage drills with specific modifications and scoring incentives to focus attention on common concerns for each defense.

Team Defensive Drill 1   **Perimeter**

Because the greatest strength of the perimeter defense is its flexibility, practice making blocking adjustments with every ball initiated. When the instructor puts the ball into play, call out "line" or "angle" and test to see whether the defense makes the correct adjustment.

TO INCREASE DIFFICULTY

- Have the blocker make the decision without telling the defense. The defense will have to read even more to line up correctly.
- Add front-row attackers to defend against.
- Encourage the setter to dump on her contact.

TO DECREASE DIFFICULTY

- Have the attacker catch the set and check defensive positions.
- Tell the attacker and defense where to attack.

Success Check

- Watch the distance of the set in relation to the block.
- Remain stationary at hitter's contact.
- Know your parallel responsibility.
- Give relentless effort to keep the ball off the floor.

Score Your Success

Earn 1 point for each correct defensive adjustment (10 attempts).

Your score ___

Team Defensive Drill 2   **Positive Point**

With both teams in rotation defense, require a specific hitter (e.g., the middle hitter) to attack the first ball. Award 1 point to the defensive team for executing the proper defensive positions and 1 point if the setter can catch the ball on balance using proper technique. Initiate the next rally with a free ball to the opposite team. Play to 10 points.

TO INCREASE DIFFICULTY

- Continue playing the point out to the end, with the coach allocating points for correct defensive positions throughout the rally.

TO DECREASE DIFFICULTY

- Have the attacker catch the ball to check defensive positions and then toss the ball to the other side and have them play it out.

Success Check

- Watch the distance of the set in relation to the block.
- Know your defensive responsibilities.
- Make every effort to keep the attack from hitting the floor.

Score Your Success

The winning team earns 10 points. The other team gets the points they earned.

Your score ___

Team Defensive Drill 3   **Defend the Seam**

Have the middle hitters on both teams commit to each other off the free ball so that they always leave a seam at the pins. The defenses should make the correct adjustments and receive 1 point for keeping the ball alive to the point of a controlled second contact. Stop the rally, score the point, and begin the next rally with a free ball to the other side. Play to 10 points.

TO INCREASE DIFFICULTY

- Allow the setter to set any front-row attacker, including the middle.
- Encourage attackers to use deception by hitting where they are not facing or using off-speed shots.
- Switch between rotation defense and perimeter.

TO DECREASE DIFFICULTY

- Designate a single attacker.
- Encourage the attacker to attack only straight through the seam.
- Continue playing the same defense.

Success Check

- Crash the seam when it is your responsibility.
- Remain stationary at contact and ready for block deflections.
- Keep the attack off the floor at all costs.

Score Your Success

Your team wins the game = 10 points

The other team wins the game = 5 points

Your score ___

Team Defensive Drill 4   **Coach on Three**

With a player at the net and three defenders in the backcourt, the instructor initiates the drill with an attacked ball into the defense. The defenders play the ball directly back to the instructor and get ready to defend another attack. Players should move from base to read on the set, dig the ball, and move back to base, and then move back into a read position. The attacker can move to any location on the net.

TO INCREASE DIFFICULTY

- Attack into the seams of the defense.
- Add a setter.
- Add multiple players ready to hit the set at different positions.

TO DECREASE DIFFICULTY

- Attack less aggressively.
- Attack directly at diggers.

Success Check

- Remain stationary at hitter's contact.
- Position your platform behind the path of the ball.
- Dig to the acceptable dig zone.

Score Your Success

Earn 1 point for each successful dig (10 attempts).

Your score ___

Team Defensive Drill 5 **Off Speed**

In this scrimmage, winning the rally earns your team 1 point, but if you get a kill with an off-speed shot, then you also get 2 bonus points. Use this scoring incentive when practicing perimeter and middle-middle defenses, the two defenses most vulnerable to off-speed shots. Play to 10 points, winning by 2.

TO INCREASE DIFFICULTY

- Provide incentive for deep off-speed shots because those are more risky.
- Reduce the players on the court to five so that fewer people need to cover more space.

TO DECREASE DIFFICULTY

- Play a rotation or man-up defense that is designed to commit a tip-coverage digger.
- Provide a point for any dug ball regardless of winning the rally.

Success Check

- Keep weight forward to pursue tips.
- Remain stationary at hitter's contact.
- Position your platform under the ball to play it high and off the net.

Score Your Success

The winning team earns 10 points for the drill. The other team gets the number of points they win, up to 10 points.

Your score ___

Team Defensive Drill 6 **Defense Switch**

Play three minigames to 3 points, with free balls to alternating sides of the net. Each team has the opportunity to switch their defense each minigame.

TO INCREASE DIFFICULTY

- Switch defenses within the minigame using hand signals.

TO DECREASE DIFFICULTY

- Focus on playing only one or two defenses.
- Focus on playing perimeter defense and change only the blocking strategy.

Success Check

- Use the tip digger's location to give you a hint of what defense your opponent is in.
- Identify your opponent's defense by recognizing which shots are dug and which are landing for kills.
- Communicate your defensive responsibilities as a team.

Score Your Success

Your team wins two or three games = 10 points

The other team wins two or three games = 5 points

Your score ___

Team Defensive Drill 7   **Game Plan**

Each team tells the other what kind of defense they are going to run. Exchange a bonus point goal for something that you feel you need to work on (e.g., off speed, using the block, defending the line). Keep track of the score and play to 10 points.

TO INCREASE DIFFICULTY

- Add more criteria for point incentives.

TO DECREASE DIFFICULTY

- Only give bonus points.

Success Check

- Stay focused on achieving your bonus while preventing the opponent's bonus.

Score Your Success

The winning team gets 10 points for the drill. The other team gets the points they earn, up to 10 points.

Your score ___

SUCCESS SUMMARY

Effective team defense depends on all six players doing their jobs and trusting each other. Regardless of whether you are a blocker or digger, covering a tip or the hard-driven ball, pursuing a deflected ball off the block or covering a setter dump, playing defense requires discipline and effort. At times you will make an incorrect read, but there's never an excuse for letting a ball hit the floor without working hard to keep it alive. As you become more familiar with the defenses described in this step, you will naturally gravitate toward one that becomes your favorite. Your favorite, however, may not be the favorite of your teammates or right against your opponent, so stay open minded and be versatile. Once you have an understanding of the principles of each defense, are comfortable in your ability to execute them, and have reached 40 points in the drills, you are ready to take the next step toward match play!

Team Defensive Drills

1. Perimeter   ___out of 10
2. Positive point   ___out of 10
3. Defend the seam   ___out of 10
4. Coach on three   ___out of 10
5. Off speed   ___out of 10
6. Defense switch   ___out of 10
7. Game plan   ___out of 10

Total   **___out of 70**

Match Play

We have discussed many of the techniques and tactics for each element of the game. The next step is to put it all together. You will learn how to assemble a team, scout an opponent, and plan a game strategy that will exploit your opponent's weaknesses and hide your own. We will discuss ways to manage the match from warm-ups to time-outs. You will learn how to read a box score and interpret the statistics of the game.

PERSONNEL

Before you can win on the court, someone has to put the team together, assign positions, establish starting rotations, and allocate playing time. This can be done by a single leader on the team or decided by committee, but it helps to have a solid understanding of the principles that go into these decisions. Success is never guaranteed, but these personnel recommendations will create an environment that increases the likelihood of success.

Putting Together a Team

Say you are in charge of putting together a team for a tournament or league. What factors are important in creating a competitive volleyball team and how should you go about determining positions? Consider these characteristics when selecting team members.

PHYSICAL CHARACTERISTICS

Because volleyball is played over a net and requires players to cover a relatively small area of the court, their height makes a big difference. In general, taller players can contact the ball higher in the air and it takes them less time to get to that height. Taller players generally have an increased wingspan, which can have a multiplying effect after considering their height (a 2-inch [5 cm] difference in height will usually mean a 4-inch [5 cm] difference in reach). Height also translates into length in the backcourt because a taller player generally has more range because of the length of his extremities. When it comes to volleyball players, size matters.

ATHLETICISM

While height is important, athleticism can make up for a lack of height. A player with a 30-inch (76 cm) vertical jump can touch higher than a player who is 5 inches (12.7 cm) taller but has only a 19-inch (48 cm) vertical jump. While height might mean a player is able to cover more linear feet of court space, it might not be enough to make up for a player who has a low center of gravity and can fly around on quick feet. Volleyball is a game in which power and finesse, strength and speed, quickness and endurance, and gross and fine motor skills are valued.

SKILL

The drills in this book have helped you develop the skills necessary to play volleyball at a high level. The challenge of volleyball is that not many skills are transferable from other sports. It takes time and practice to learn the art of serving, passing, setting, attacking, and digging. Think about the specific volleyball skills a player brings to your team; those should be considered over general athletic ability.

KNOWLEDGE

While it may not be feasible to test a player's volleyball IQ before asking her to join your team, you should consider her playing experience and understanding of the rules. Increased understanding of the rules allows greater specialization, which can help a player who is below average in physicality, athleticism, and skill to do a job that has to be done well.

ATTITUDE

Having fun while competing to win and being active should be the goal of any sport. Think about the personalities your teammates bring to the team and if they will make an emotional investment or withdraw from the team dynamic. About twice as much time is spent between rallies as is spent in rallies. During that time, your teammates' personalities will come out.

Assigning Positions

When determining which position each person will play, certain characteristics lend themselves to some positions over others. Of course, these are not universal, but they can be helpful in putting players in positions to be successful rather than setting them up for failure. Each is also described with an occupation that characterizes the kind of contribution they make on the court.

PLAYER POSITIONS AND OCCUPATIONS

Setter: The general who leads the offense

The setter has to understand the game plan and know how to facilitate the offensive success of the team. She has to be able to cover the entire court.

Left-side hitter: The artist who takes something such as a bad pass and makes something great out of it.

In general, she will get the majority of the sets. She should be able to balance aggressiveness with smarts by not hitting balls out that are poorly set. Most common hitter that plays across both the front and back rows.

Middle hitter: The workhorse who has to do a lot of work but doesn't get noticed much.

The middle hitter's responsibilities include attempting to double block on every hit by the opponent and running a first-tempo attack whenever the ball is set. Watch a middle hitter instead of the ball during a high-level match and you will be tired just from watching.

Right-side hitter: The magician who catches defenses off guard.

One of the primary responsibilities of the right side is to be a strong enough blocker to stop or slow an opponent's top left side. The right-side position is gaining recognition because of the ability to surprise the opponent with an attack the opponent doesn't typically see. Attacks coming from the right side are usually more difficult for the defense to handle. Because many right-side hitters are left-handed, they have the advantage because they give the defense a different style arm swing to worry about.

Libero (defensive specialist): The mailperson who has to be consistent in her role as the middleman between the opponent and the setter.

The libero has three main responsibilities: pass the serve, dig balls, and cover hitters. Typically, liberos also bring excitement and energy to the court that can add to the team's feeling of momentum.

MISSTEP

You put your best player in a position other than setter.

CORRECTION

The setter gets the opportunity to influence almost every play, and your best player should perform that role. The big hitters get the glory and it certainly is fun to hit hard, but the setting position is the key to success.

Establishing a Lineup

When putting together a lineup, you should consider several factors. Players are labeled by position, and rotations are determined by the location of the setter. Specific player positions are opposite each other so that players who play the same position are not in the front or back row together at the same time. Substitutions may be made for any player, but they must maintain their rotational order. When running a 6-2, the setter starts in zone 1, followed in zone 2 by a left-side hitter, a middle hitter in zone 3, and in zone 4 another setter or right side. Because players must be opposite, the other left-side hitter would be in zone 5 followed by the other middle in zone 6 (figure 9.1). In the 6-2, pay special attention to which hitters work best off which setters. Because each hitter (other than the right side) will be in the front row for three rotations, two of them will be with one setter and one of them will be with the other. Often hitters are more successful off one setter than the other; be sure to consider this when assigning positions. In figure 9.1, players are identified with a number corresponding to the setter they will have for two rotations.

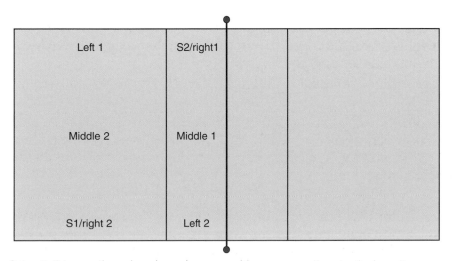

Figure 9.1 6-2 formation showing player positions according to their setter.

When you are running a 5-1, you can set your lineup in two primary ways. The middle-lead lineup (figure 9.2a) puts the middle hitter in zone 6 when the setter is in zone 1. In the left-lead lineup, the left-side hitter is in zone 6 when the setter is in zone 1 (figure 9.2b). These are identified by these names because of the position that leads the setter. The middle-lead lineup is the most common because of the ease with which the L2 can be used in serve-receive systems. Remembering the overlap rules, many unique patterns can be created to showcase your best passers and get the best matchups between your hitters and the blockers. See figure 9.2 for ideas for designing serve-receive patterns.

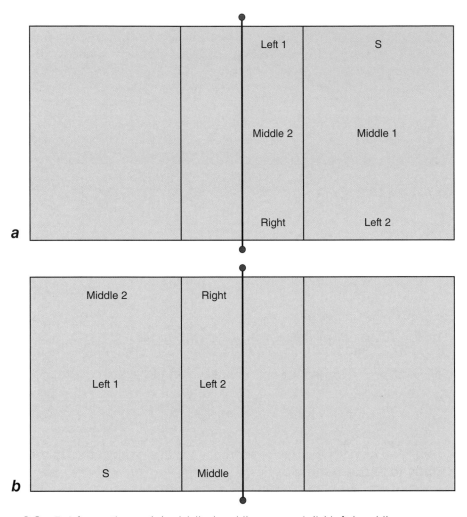

Figure 9.2 5-1 formations: *(a)* middle-lead lineup and *(b)* left-lead lineup.

Most of the time you will surround your setter with your best middle and your best left side. By doing this you only have your best hitters in the front row at the same time for one rotation (the rotation when the setter is also in the front row). Reconsider this when you have a middle who is good at the slide attack. Even if she is not your best hitter, you might want to put her in the M1 position because that position hits the slide in two rotations and the M2 hits the slide in only one rotation.

MISSTEP

You placed your two best hitters next to each other in the rotation.

CORRECTION

You don't want your best two hitters stealing sets from each other, which would happen if you put them next to each other. Place them either opposite each other or on both sides of the setter.

Starting Rotation

A couple philosophies influence the rotation a team should start in. This is an important decision because whichever rotation a team starts in will be the rotation they are in the most. In most matches, a team will complete three full rotations. If you happen to go a few more times than that, make sure you use your most successful rotations. Most teams simply rotate their lineups so that their best hitter starts in the left front. When running a 5-1, many start their setter in the right back so that they have three blockers for the first three rotations. More advanced teams evaluate statistics on the percentage of points that they win in each rotation and start there. Carefully consider starting rotation in order to make sure that you maximize your scoring opportunities. In a game decided by 2 points, every point counts.

Substitutions

Substitutions allow for greater specialization or the opportunity to give a player a rest. Some levels of the game restrict the number of substitutions to 12, while others are unlimited. There are no reentry limitations, except at the Olympic level, but once you go into the match at one position, you cannot go in for a player in another spot in the rotation.

Consider using substitutions as a part of your normal rotation

- if you have one or two players who are deficient in either the front or back row,
- if you are running a 6-2 and want to replace your back-row setter with a hitter when he or she gets to the front row,
- or if you have a blocking or serving specialist who comes into the match only to perform those duties.

You might also consider subbing when a particular player is struggling or as a way to break momentum when the opponent goes on a run.

MISSTEP

You taking a player out when he makes a couple of errors.

CORRECTION

While every point is important, subbing after one or two errors channels players into playing out of fear. Not only will this result in players being tentative, it also will create a tension-filled environment on the court.

SCOUTING THE OPPONENT

The scouting reports that college teams put together on their opponents contain vast numbers of statistics, charts, and tendencies. Because teams can look different from one rotation to the next, scouting reports usually are broken down by rotation to provide a more accurate glimpse of an opponent's tendencies. Scouting the opponent does not have to be complicated, but it is beneficial to know something about your opponent. Noting the information described here might be overkill for your team and at your level, but understanding the process of scouting can help you have a greater understanding of how the game is played and won.

Offense and Defense Type

Start by identifying the opponent's offensive and defensive systems. If they are running a 5-1, then identify whether or not the setter is an offensive threat. If they are running a 6-2, then identify their setting strategy for when the setter takes the first ball. If the secondary setter is not very good, attack to the right back as often as possible.

You also want to identify the type of defense they are playing so that you understand where the seams are and how to exploit the weaknesses. No defense equally defends the entire court and each exposes vulnerabilities. Finding those systematic vulnerabilities as well as identifying players who are stronger or weaker will help you know where to attack.

Serve-Receive Patterns

In each rotation, specific serve-receive patterns are carefully designed to minimize weaknesses and exploit strengths. Knowing what a team is trying to accomplish in each of those patterns will put you in a much better position to defend it. Charting where the attackers are in the pattern and what types of sets they are hitting can help your blockers know whether or not to commit to specific hitters or what kind of defense would be best to run.

Offensive Tendencies

It is the rare attacker who can hit every spot on the court with the same accuracy and power. Most hitters are better at some shots than others and show those tendencies in their play. Keeping a simple shot chart of each hitter can reveal where they like to attack and what attacks are most effective. Remember that just because it is effective against one team doesn't mean it will be effective against another.

MISSTEP

You have not developed a full arsenal of shots.

CORRECTION

Having multiple shots at your disposal will prevent opponents from scouting you and creating a defensive strategy that limits your effectiveness.

Serving Targets

While most teams will intentionally put only strong passers in their serve-receive patterns, one area of the court is usually a better target than others. Identifying a poor passer in the pattern is the first step a server takes when determining where to target his serve. If all of the passers are equally strong, then serving to different locations can put pressure on different aspects of the opponent's offense. For instance, serving to zone 1 results in poor sets to the left side because it puts pressure on the setter to square up to the left antenna. Serving to zone 5 makes it difficult for the quick middle attacker to track the pass and be on time. If the opponent is effective at running a crossing play, then serve short to congest the area where the hitters are crossing. If none of those tactics work, then serve a low, deep ball to the back 3 feet (1 m) of the court to make it more challenging to pass tight to the net and run a quick offense.

Vulnerabilities

Identifying systematic and personnel vulnerabilities can open up options to your offense. If you notice that a particular player is a weak blocker or digger, then your hitters should exploit that weakness. If you realize that the opponent is running a rover defense and the middles are not proficient at closing the block, then your pin hitters should attack the seam to zone 6. If the opponent's setter struggles to back set, then move your left-side blocker's base position to the right so that it is easier to double block the middle. Remember that every point you score is also a point that your opponent doesn't. Maximize your opportunity to win by taking advantage of your opponent's vulnerabilities.

Common Game Plan Approaches

A few strategies are effective against most teams. Even if you don't have a scouting report or have never seen the team that you are playing, these tactics usually lead to a few points.

ATTACK THE SETTER (RIGHT BACK)

Forcing the setter to make the first contact usually eliminates the opponent's quick middle attack. Your block can then set up against the pin hitter and you are much more likely to score the point.

ATTACK THE SIDELINE DIGGER ON THE SIDELINE

One of the fundamental rules of being a crosscourt digger is to stay on your line until you are sure your hitter cannot make the shot. If your opponent is not disciplined, they will leave the sideline and expose an extremely vulnerable area of the court. From the antennae, this means attacking the sharp crosscourt where the 10-foot (3 m) line meets the sideline.

RISK VS. REWARD

Even good teams hit the ball out of bounds about 10 percent of the time. This means that just by keeping the ball in play, you are 10 percent closer to scoring a point. Don't take unnecessary risks just for the sake of playing aggressively. Force your opponent to make more mistakes than you do by staying disciplined and keeping the ball in play.

ESTABLISH THE MIDDLE ATTACK AND SETTER DUMP EARLY

Even if the ball doesn't go down for a kill, establishing the quick middle attack and setter dump holds the blockers and prevents them from thinking that they can leave early to block at a pin. This strategy helps you consistently realize seams in the block for both the middle attack and those at the pins.

MATCH MANAGEMENT

Different levels of volleyball use different warm-up protocols. Make sure you know the protocol, as well as your physical needs and those of your teammates, to ensure that you are prepared to play your best at the first serve. Typically, a series of arm circles, lunges, jogging, jumps, squats, jacks, stretches, and push-ups will warm up the body enough to prepare it for exercise. Although your team has only your side of the net on which to warm up, use the space by doing partner ball-control work or team defense drills (e.g., coach on three).

The college game includes two warm-up periods during which each team uses the whole court. Most teams use the first segment for serve and serve-receive work and use the second segment for attacking. Some protocols allow shared court time only when both teams attack at the same time on their side of the net. When this is the case, announce when you are attacking from anywhere other than the left antenna and avoid your opponents by attacking to locations void of waiting attackers.

Calling a time-out can be a way to break your opponent's momentum or change a strategy in order to gain an advantage. Even recreational teams are given at least one time-out each set, but most teams are given two. Because volleyball is a game in which momentum plays a significant role, it is best to call a time-out earlier rather than later. It has also been shown that the team that gets to point 16 first wins the set significantly more often, which is evidence against holding onto your time-outs until later in the set. When you call a time-out, don't try to give too much information or be so vague that everyone has a different interpretation of what you said. Give no more than three simple instructions or adjustments, identify what has been effective for you or your opponent, or simply find a way to help your team find the right emotional level to perform at their best.

MISSTEP

You called a time-out on game point.

CORRECTION

Use your time-outs early to influence the match. Sometimes calling a time-out can make your team even more nervous. Often, a time-out on game point is too late to make a difference.

UNDERSTANDING STATISTICS

A lot can be learned about a match from looking at the box score and interpreting statistics. The statistics in the box score are defined here, as well as other statistics commonly taken by coaches. We also discuss ways to interpret the statistics to evaluate player and team performance.

BOX SCORE STATISTICS

- *Matches and sets*: The number of matches (M) and sets (S) played regardless of how much time was spent in the match or whether or not they achieved any recorded statistics.

- *Hits*: Total attempts (TA) refers to the number of times a player hits, tips, and sets the ball strategically over the net with the intent to score. Kills (K) are earned anytime an attack is unreturnable by the opponent or directly causes an opponent's net violation. Attacking errors (E) are charged to a hitter anytime he or she hits the ball out of bounds, is blocked to the floor, attacks into the net (resulting in a four-hit violation), or hits the ball into the antenna. The hitter earns an attacking error when he or she contacts the ball illegally, crosses the centerline, or commits a back-row attack violation. Hitting percentage is calculated by subtracting errors from kills and dividing by total attempts ($[K - E] \div TA$). Strong hitters often get 3.0 kills per set and .300+ hitting efficiency.

- *Assists*: An assist (A) is earned by a player anytime he or she passes, sets, or digs a ball that is immediately followed by a kill. Strong setters typically average 10.0+ assists per set.

- *Serves*: A service ace (SA) is earned by a player when a serve directly results in a point because of the opponent's inability to keep the ball in play or a violation of rotation order. A service error (SE) is earned when a player contacts a serve illegally or the ball fails to land in the opponent's court. A strong server will typically average .75 aces per set.

- *Reception errors*: Reception errors (RE) are charged to players when they fail to pass a serve with a legal contact or in such a way that their teammates cannot keep the ball in play. Reception errors should equal opponent's aces. Reception errors is a misleading statistic if you don't also know the number of reception attempts.

- *Digs*: A dig (D) is awarded to a player when he is able to pass an attacked ball. Strong liberos typically average 5.0 digs per set, and three-rotation back-row players average 2.5+.

- *Blocks*: A solo block (SB) is awarded to a single player who blocks an attacked ball back to the floor for a point. A block assist (BA) is earned by both players who jump and block a ball to the floor for a point. A blocking error (BE) is charged to a player who contacts the net or antenna or violates the centerline while blocking. A back-row player who blocks (commonly a setter) is also charged a blocking error for the fault. Outstanding middle blockers typically average 1.0 block per set, and strong pin blockers earn .7 blocks per set.

- *Ball-handling errors*: Anytime a player commits a lift or double contact, she is charged with a ball-handling error (BHE).

- *Points*: All of the statistics that immediately result in points (kills, aces, and blocks) are added together to reveal total points (TP).

MISSTEP

You counted a covered block as a dig.

CORRECTION

A player who covers a block is not rewarded with an official statistic because the block was not an attack (a critical part of the dig definition).

OTHER STATISTICS

- *Side-out percentage* refers to how often a team is able to win a point when receiving serve. This statistic is highly correlated with winning, and good teams side out at 70 percent or higher.
- *Serve-receive statistics* are evaluated on a 4-point scale and were explained in step 2, but that same scale can be used to evaluate the effectiveness of a serve. Just as a passer would strive to get a 3-point pass, a server tries to get the opponent to pass a zero

It is possible to learn a lot about a match from looking at the box score. Besides seeing how close the games were or whether or not the match went three sets or five, a nuanced eye can learn a lot from the statistics. Offensively, look at the difference in hitting percentage between the two teams and look at whether or not the difference in hitting percentage came from increased kills for the leading team or increased errors for the losing team. Identifying the positions of the players with the most attempts can tell you the quality of passing. If the middles received a lot of attacking attempts, then the passing must have been good enough to get them the ball. Look at the number of assists to tell what kind of offense the teams are running. Two players with similar assist numbers reveals a two-setter offense (either 6-2 or 4-2), while a 5-1 shows one setter with the vast majority of sets. Looking at side-out percentage can tell you whether or not the match was close throughout or whether teams scored points by going on serving runs.

Match Play Drill 1   **Assigning Teams**

You can use a variety of methods to create teams. Lining up players by height and counting off assures that the teams will be well balanced vertically. The volleyball version of letting free throws determine pickup basketball teams is to serve or attack into a designated zone. The first six players to hit the zone make up the first team. As the competitive level improves, more position specialization can occur and players can play the same positions with rotating teammates. Use the following methods for assigning teams and scrimmage to 15 points:

- Height (tallest to shortest).
- Age (oldest to youngest).
- Volleyball experience (most to least).
- Hometown (alphabetical).
- Academic interest (alphabetical).

Find out which method results in the closest matches.

TO INCREASE DIFFICULTY

- Group participants by ability and have the stronger groups play each other and the weaker groups play each other.
- Have participants submit a draft of teams based on the criteria described in this step.

TO DECREASE DIFFICULTY

- Make teams completely random.
- Switch players from team to team between matches.

Success Check

- No matter who is on your team, find ways to maximize your chances of success.
- Communicate about what you are doing and what your opponent is doing.
- Give maximal effort.

Score Your Success

Win three or more games to 15 = 10 points

Win one or two games to 15 = 6 points

Win no games to 15 = 2 points

Your score ___

Match Play Drill 2   **Continuous Rally**

The objective of this drill is to overtrain the pace of the game to improve decision making and control. With six players on each side of the net in base defensive positions, place two additional players with a supply of balls behind the middle-back defender (figure 9.3). Play is initiated by a free ball and the rally continues until the ball is dead. A toss is made to the setter on the same side of the dead ball to simulate a dig and play resumes. Keep score (even though play resumes quickly) and teams play to 10 points, winning by 2 points.

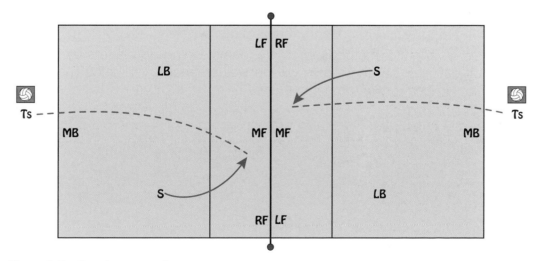

Figure 9.3   Continuous rally.

(continued)

Match Play Drill 2 *(continued)*

TO INCREASE DIFFICULTY

- Toss the continuation ball into the drill quickly

TO DECREASE DIFFICULTY

- Give teams time to get set before initiating the continuation ball.

Success Check

- Remember what worked against your opponent and what didn't.
- Focus on technique when you get tired.
- Communicate throughout the rally.

Score Your Success

You get the number of points that your team earned, up to a maximum of 10.

Your score ___

Match Play Drill 3   U-S-A

The objective of this drill is to earn three points in a row. The drill begins with one team serving to the other in rotational order. The team that wins that rally calls out "U" and gets a free ball. If they win that rally, then they yell out "S" and get another free ball. If the other team wins the rally, they yell out "U" and get the free ball. This continues until one team wins U-S-A by getting three points in a row. Teams switch front-row and back-row players and play again. If the teams split wins, then a third game is played with each team determining who they want in each position.

TO INCREASE DIFFICULTY

- Find an acronym that is four letters long to extend the drill.
- Change team defense between points.
- Teams can also start in rotation (as if they would be playing a normal game) and both teams rotate every time a U-S-A is scored.

TO DECREASE DIFFICULTY

- Require only two consecutive rally wins to earn a point.
- Allow players to stay in their positions from game to game to gain comfort.

Success Check

- Swing hard when you have an advantage, but be conservative when you don't.
- Exploit vulnerabilities in your opponent.
- Finish by being smart in pressure situations.

Your team wins two or three games = 10 points

Your team wins one game = 5 points

Your team wins no games = 2 points

Your score ___

Match Play Drill 4   Steal the Bacon

Two teams in base defensive position play out seven balls, keeping track of the score. Whichever team wins 4 points or more has the opportunity to choose whether they want to serve or receive. If that team wins the rally, then they get all the points from the first seven balls. If the other team wins the served-ball rally, they get a free-ball opportunity to steal the points from the opponent. If they lose, then neither team scores points. Rotate and continue to play to 25 points.

TO INCREASE DIFFICULTY

- Play best of nine balls.
- The team that wins the most out of the seven balls *must* serve and win that rally to earn their points.

TO DECREASE DIFFICULTY

- Play best of five balls.
- Play to 15 points.

Success Check

- Establish defensive and offensive systems.
- Start in your best rotations.
- Call a time-out if struggling.

Score Your Success

Your team wins = 10 points

The other team wins = 5 points

Your score ___

SUCCESS SUMMARY

Step by step you learned the skills of volleyball and how to use them successfully. Now you have learned how to put all the skills together. From using a variety of characteristics to put a team together to putting them in the right places on the court, you have learned how to manage a team to victory. You have learned how to identify vulnerabilities in your opponent and maximize the strengths of your team. You understand how to evaluate skills within the game using statistics so that you can gain a deeper understanding of your team's success or what is holding you back. It is my hope that you will take this knowledge and positively influence the players with whom you are competing. When you feel confident making these decisions and tactical adjustments in the drills and have earned 28 points or more, then you are well on your way to mastering the game of volleyball! In the next step, you will learn about the variations of the game that require a diverse array of skills and adaptability.

Match Play Drills

1.	Assigning teams	___out of 10
2.	Continuous rally	___out of 10
3.	U-S-A	___out of 10
4.	Steal the bacon	___out of 10
	Total	___**out of 40**

Variations

"Volley Ball is a new game which is pre-eminently fitted for the gymnasium or the exercise hall, but which may also be played out-of-doors. Any number of persons may play the game."

This quote from the original rules of volleyball in the *Official Handbook of the Young Men's Christian Associations of North America* appeared early in the book. As you can gather, William Morgan envisioned a game that was adaptable. That flexibility in numbers and context has contributed to volleyball's worldwide success and popularity.

This step provides an overview of the many popular variations on the game so that you will be confident participating across multiple venues and formats, including sand, coed, grass, sitting, wallyball, and footvolley. A separate book could be written for each of these disciplines, but it is the intent of this step to provide you with a brief introduction to the differences in rules and techniques involved in each.

SAND

The explosion of sand volleyball in the 1980s resulted in its inclusion as a sport in the Olympic Summer Games in 1996. Currently in the United States, there are more than 40 women's sand volleyball programs in the NCAA, and club programs all over the country are developing high school programs to provide scholarship-eligible student-athletes.

Most sand tournaments are for doubles teams, while others can include triples, fours, or sixes. A doubles court is 26 feet, 3 inches × 52 feet, 6 inches (8 m × 16 m) and the net height for men and women (as well as court dimensions for teams larger than two players) are the same as for indoor volleyball. While antennae may be used at the court boundary, most sand players use the extension of the poles as antennae. A sand court has no center line, and players are allowed to cross into the opponent's court as long as they do not interfere with the opponent's ability to play the ball or touch the net.

According to USA Volleyball sand volleyball rules, a match consists of winning two out of three sets, with the first two sets to 21 points and the third, deciding set (if necessary) played to 15 points. Teams switch sides every 7 points in order to eliminate a wind or sun advantage. In sand volleyball, serving order must be maintained, players have no positional requirements as in indoor volleyball. Contact by the blocker is considered one of the three contacts allowed a team; however, the blocker is allowed to play the second contact. A player may only double contact a hard-driven attack (not allowed on the serve), so it is recommended that beach players use their forearms to dig as often as possible. Setting is judged more strictly outdoors than indoors and players should be disciplined in releasing a set with very little spin. To do so, sand players usually use an extended pause when contacting the ball during the set, while others simply use forearm passing to avoid a double-contact violation. Anytime a player uses an overhead setting technique, the ball must travel in the direction his shoulders are facing. When attacking the ball, sand players are not allowed to use an open-hand tip with relaxed fingers. The player must poke the ball with either stiff fingers or the knuckles.

The sand, sun, and wind can present challenges not seen indoors. When indoor players first play in the sand, they tend to be early on their approach to attack because they expect to jump higher. The tendency is also to hit with the same power as indoor. With a smaller court and less jumping ability, it is wise to use strategic shots, such as roll shots along the net or pokes to the deep corners, as the power game is developed. Be sure your passes and sets are high enough, but not so high that the wind takes them away from your target. Blocking can be a strong defensive move against a powerful hitter but it requires careful timing and communication. The same principle affecting the timing of an attack will affect your block. Be sure to wait until just after the hitter jumps to begin your blocking jump. If the opposing attacker is not a power-hitting threat, don't waste half of your defense on a strategy that will work only once or twice a match. Instead, keep both players back, reading the attacker's arm swing.

The first strategy you need to consider is how to prevent your opponents from performing the skills at which they are most talented. Which player is the better passer, setter, or attacker? Remember that in doubles, every time you play the ball to the opponent you can dictate who will have to pass, set, and attack back at you. If one of your opponents is a much better hitter than the other, it makes sense to serve the weaker hitter. If one player is a weaker setter, then play the ball to the partner so that it forces your opponent to play into her weakness.

The learning curve for defensive positioning in the sand is steep. When your teammate is serving, position yourself near the net and in the middle of the court. If there is an overpass, then you are in a perfect position to make the play. If you have decided to block, then signal to your partner whether you intend to take line or angle from each hitter on the other side. Showing your index finger to your partner indicates taking line and showing your index and middle finger means that you will be blocking angle. Your partner will move to the side of the court that is being given to the attacker. If the ball is set far off the net, then blocking becomes less valuable and you should peel off the net into the side of the court that you were going to take away with your block. When neither player intends to block, the player nearest the net peels off to a read position on his or her side of the court. The player on the same side of the court as the hitter generally takes a couple steps forward to prepare for the roll shot right over the net, while the crosscourt digger prepares to defend the hard-driven ball. When a team has a single player who is very good at blocking and one who is a better digger, you will see them commit to those responsibilities regardless of who is serving. Blockers may change their tactics in the middle of a rally by showing their hand signal to their partner behind their back. One of the significant differences in sand volleyball is that the players getting ready to dig have to read the opposing hitter and start moving in the direction they think the hitter will attack. When playing indoors, defensive players want to be stationary at the hitter's contact, but if you try that strategy in the sand you often will be late to the ball. This means that, on occasion, you will guess wrong, but as your reading ability improves, so will the number of balls you are able to chase down.

Successful offenses use several basic tactics. When a team is not blocking you and the quality of set allows you to take an aggressive swing at the ball, try to attack between the defenders. Going for the middle of the court might cause both players to extend to make the play; even if one is capable of getting the ball up, the other will be out of position to make the second contact. If a team is not blocking and employs the defensive strategy outlined previously in this step (crosscourt digger back with line digger short), then a sharp crosscourt roll shot that runs the length of the net will be effective. This shot is also difficult to attack without putting the ball so high that the defenders are able to run it down, so low that it never crosses the net, or so hard that it lands out of bounds on the sideline. Practicing this shot so that it is a consistent part of your arsenal will create more problems for the defensive team than simply being able to hit a hard crosscourt shot. When a team is blocking you, hit a high shot into the area of the court in the shadow of the block.

Make sure that you are prepared for playing in the elements. Sunglasses protect your eyes from both the sun and the sand that might fly off the ball as you play it. Short sand time-outs are allowed, so have a towel on hand to wipe off sand between points. Be sure to drink plenty of water because cramping is much more common in sand tournaments than indoors. Be prepared for weather fluctuations because the only time that sand volleyball games are cancelled is when the court is unsafe because of lightning, blowing debris, and so on.

Common etiquette on the sand volleyball court includes getting most of the sand off the ball before you toss it to another player, acknowledging that you are screening a server and move to the side, calling out the score before every serve (your score first), and acknowledging your own rule violations when you commit them. Most sand games don't have a referee. Even if there is a referee, it is on each player to call his or her own illegal contacts and net violations. Sand volleyball is a community game with players switching partners between games and putting the quality of the game on a higher pedestal than an individual winning record. Consistently overpassing a set when both players are back digging, for instance, is a strategy that can result in winning points but does not respect the game. When considering the ethics of a competitive strategy, use the Golden Rule (treat others as you would like to be treated) and you will create a competitive environment that is challenging and fun. And a final word of advice: always dive for a ball with your mouth closed.

COED AND REVERSE COED

Volleyball is a game that is often played with both sexes on the same team. While the volleyball rules that govern these games are usually consistent with single-sex games, some differences are specific to individual leagues or tournaments. When the match is played using a net at the men's height, here are common rule changes to accommodate a coed structure:

- Ratio of men to women on the court at the same time (usually 3:3).
- Positions of men and women on the court in relationship to each other (usually staggered: male, female, male, female, and so on).
- Ball contact by a female member of the team; usually a female teammate must contact the ball at least once unless the team does not use all three contacts (many teams use a female setter to satisfy this rule).

Because the game is played with the net at the men's height, coed tournaments often cause women to feel less valued on the team. Reverse coed tournaments were developed to provide the opportunity for men and women to play together but use a net at the women's height. To eliminate the height advantage that men have on a women's net, men are allowed to jump and attack the ball only from behind the 10-foot (3 m) line and are not allowed to jump and block. In regular coed matches, one woman must touch the ball when using three contacts to play the ball over; in a reverse coed match, one man must be responsible for a contact.

GRASS

Grass volleyball is a popular option for both recreational and competitive players. It is easier to set up a volleyball net system in grass than it is in sand, and any park, yard, or soccer field (even golf course) can offer enough space to run multiple courts for a tournament.

The rules for grass volleyball most often match those used in sand. The main difference in grass volleyball is that usually players can be a little quicker and more explosive than in the sand. You probably won't realize the same timing issues as in the sand, but it will still be different from indoors. Grass tournaments are usually triples, fours, or sixes, but with no 10-foot (3 m) line, back-row players must call their own illegal attacks when too close to the net.

When playing with three players, all can attack in the front row, and players should defend in the three lanes in which they start. If you want to block, designate one blocker to take away the middle back of the court and have the two wing defenders dig the line and sharp crosscourt shots.

When playing fours, most leagues and tournaments require one player to be in the back row and every player will rotate through this position. Keep a single blocker devoted to blocking all front-row hitters and allocate one digger to the line and one to the crosscourt while allowing the back-row player the opportunity to read around the block.

SITTING

The Paralympic version of volleyball involves each competitor keeping one "cheek" (one side of the buttocks) on the floor at all times and is played on a court 16 feet, 5 inches × 39 feet, 4 inches (5 m × 12 m) and divided by a net set to 3 feet, 9 inches (1.15 m) for men and 3 feet, 5 inches (1.05 m) for women (figure 10.1). Most of the indoor volleyball rules for standing players are used in sitting volleyball with a few variations:

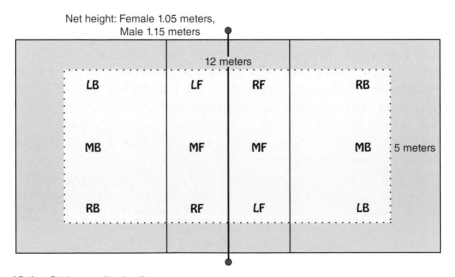

Figure 10.1 Sitting volleyball.

- Players must maintain contact with the floor at all times except for a brief moment when making a defensive play.

- The serve comes from the right-back area of the court and the player's buttocks must be entirely behind the end line (the legs can cross the line).

- An attack may be attempted at any height as long as contact remains between the player's buttocks and the floor and a back-row player's buttocks is entirely behind the 6-foot, 7-inch (2 m) attack line.

- Players may switch into specialized positions, but contact between their buttocks and the floor must be maintained.

- Blocking is allowed by front-row players as long as contact between the player's buttocks and the floor is maintained.

Sitting volleyball is not just for athletes with lower-body amputations. Any player with a physical disability is allowed to play sitting volleyball and the game can be a way to provide an adapted and inclusive competitive opportunity to bring athletes with and without disabilities together.

WALLYBALL

Wallyball is a variation of volleyball played in a racquetball court divided by a net that connects to eyebolts inserted into the side walls. The ball is the same size as an official volleyball and made out of the same blue rubber as a racquetball. Teams consist of two to six players per side and follow the same position alignments as outlined in the section on grass volleyball.

A team wins a match by winning two of three or three of five sets. Each set is played to 15 points and uses a hybrid of rally and side-out scoring. Until the serving team reaches the freeze point (3 points less than what is needed to win, usually 12 points), rally scoring is used, with a point being scored on each serve. After the freeze point, side-out scoring goes into effect for both teams (a team scores a point only when they win a rally that they served). The team winning a set has to achieve a 2-point advantage.

Play initiates with a serve from anywhere within 3 feet (1 m) of the back wall of the court. Each team gets three contacts to play the ball over the net without the ball hitting the ceiling, back wall, or two consecutive walls on the opponent's side before contacting the floor or a player. A rally ends when the ball contacts the floor on a team's side, an illegal contact is committed, or the ball is played out of bounds. The ball cannot strike the back wall before a team's contact (out of bounds), but a team can use the back wall or side walls to redirect the ball to other players or across the net. Using an overhead passing technique is illegal in wallyball, but blocking or attacking the serve is permitted. As in sand and grass volleyball, open-hand tipping is illegal.

Wallyball is a fast-paced game. It can take time to learn to use the sidewalls to redirect attacks and read the angles of the game. When attacking, it is beneficial to keep the ball along the sidewalls by attacking hard and low (where the floor and wall meet) or attacking soft and high on the wall so that the ball stays close to the wall as it drops. Attacking the ball near the deep wall can keep your opponent from having enough space to defend the ball well, but it comes with the risk of going deep. Wallyball is a fun game using typical volleyball skills and tactics in a condensed area and at fast speeds.

FOOTVOLLEY

If you have ever been to Copacabana Beach in Rio de Janeiro, Brazil, you may have seen groups of people playing volleyball in the sand only to realize that they were using their feet, chests, and heads to play the ball instead of their arms. Footvolley is a sport that blends sand volleyball with soccer. Teams (usually doubles) play on the courts the same size as sand volleyball but on a net 6 feet, 7 inches (2 m) high, regardless of sex, and use a size 5 soccer ball. Players are not allowed to contact the ball with any part of their arms, but virtually every other rule follows those of volleyball. The only other exception is that players in footvolley can contact the net without losing a point. When a player scores a bicycle kick (both feet off the ground with the kicking foot above the head), 2 points are awarded. Games are played to 25 points.

ADAPTED GAMES FOR YOUTH AND NOVICE PLAYERS

While volleyball is a popular sport at the high school, college, and adult levels in the United States, it is not popular as a youth sport. Volleyball has been slower than sports such as soccer, basketball, baseball, softball, and hockey at making developmental adaptations to its rules and equipment in order to facilitate the competence of young players. Recently, however, programs have begun using lighter balls, lower nets, smaller courts, and fewer players in order to increase the number of contacts for each player as well as their perceived responsibility in covering the court. You may find yourself coaching or teaching a youth team and will use these adaptations to help young people understand the concepts and skills of this game in a way that helps them succeed. In fact, these adaptations may be effective for novice adult players as well. Changing the court dimensions, ball size, net height, and nature of the contacts allows young players to be more successful in the game and encourages them to continue playing.

Newcomb

This game teaches the concepts of volleyball but in a slower and more controlled setting. Instead of requiring the ball to rebound on each contact, players are allowed to catch and throw the ball. Teams are allowed three contacts per side. If the ball lands in bounds on an opponent's side of the net, the attacking team gets a point. Throwing the ball out of bounds or contacting the net results in a point for the opponent. The game uses side-out scoring and is played to 11 points.

Volley-Tots

This adaptation is ideal for children 6 to 10 years old. Using a portable net system with a height between 4 and 5 feet (1.2-1.5 m), divide a standard volleyball court lengthwise so that it becomes three courts (each court is about 20 feet × 15 feet [6 × 4.6 m]). Skills are taught in practice, but when it comes to playing games, players are put into teams of four. Regular serving rotation and rally scoring are used, but players are allowed to catch the first two contacts.

The teammate who catches the second contact tosses the ball up to a teammate who uses an approach to jump and attack the ball over the net. If the other team is able to prevent it from touching the ground, then the rally continues and they use the same progression of contacts. As players advance, the teams are required to catch only the second contact. Using a pass and attack but allowing the caught second ball adds enough control while encouraging players to use all three contacts on their side. Play games to 15 points and encourage players to play with different teammates.

Minivolley

This is the next progression of volley-tots; players are required to use volleyball skills for all contacts but on a smaller court (approximately 15-20 feet square for each side of the net) using a lighter ball and a lower net (approximately 6-6.5 feet high). There is flexibility in the court size to allow for sport directors to facilitate the most success of their participants. This game is appropriate for children ages 11 to 13. Play games to 15 and teams can either remain the same from match to match or switch.

Variation Drill 1   Split-Court Doubles

Place an antenna in the middle of the net, dividing the court into two long sections. Place cones or markers to create a line separating the two (figure 10.2). Play a doubles game, with one partner receiving serve in the backcourt and the other partner setting in the frontcourt. The opponents should have one player blocking while the other reads around the block to dig. Play the rally out using rally scoring.

Teams switch who they are playing and compete with new partners. Teams can even play crosscourt. Keep track of who can win most often regardless of whom their partner is or whom they are playing against. Play to 10 points (winning by 2) and then find a new partner and pair to play. Play three matches total with and against different people every time.

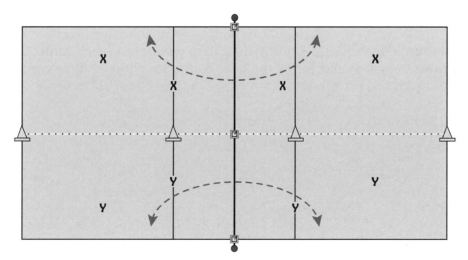

Figure 10.2 Split-court doubles.

(continued)

Variation Drill 1 *(continued)*

TO INCREASE DIFFICULTY

- Play diagonally to the crosscourt.
- Switch positions every time you play the ball over the net.

TO DECREASE DIFFICULTY

- Play with the same partner to get more comfortable.
- Use off-speed and roll shots to maintain control.

Success Check

- Hit the direction you face.
- Communicate with your partner.

Score Your Success

25 to 30 points earned = 10 points

15 to 24 points earned = 5 points

14 or fewer points earned = 2 points

Your score ___

Variation Drill 2   **Speedball**

Speedball is a game perfect for doubles or triples and uses the entire court. Two teams start on the court opposite each other with one team serving. The team that loses the rally leaves the court and is replaced by a team ready to serve behind them. In this game, the winning side always receives serve. Play for five minutes and have players keep track of their wins. Players can keep the same partner or find a new one every time they lose.

TO INCREASE DIFFICULTY

- Allow players to attack from anywhere on the court.
- Permit open-hand tips.

TO DECREASE DIFFICULTY

- Allow only back-row attacks.
- Do not allow tips.

Success Check

- Always be ready.
- Exploit weaknesses in your opponent.
- Communicate with your partner.

Score Your Success

15 wins or more = 10 points

8 to 14 wins = 5 points

7 or fewer points = 1 point

Your score ___

Variation Drill 3 **Redemption**

In step 4 on attacking, this drill was used to develop tactics by teaching players to take strategic risks. However, the game is also a fun variation to play.

This game can be played with any number of players on the court and requires an instructor or off player. Toss a ball to a team to start the rally. When a player makes a mistake, the instructor re-creates the same type of ball that caused the error, giving the player an opportunity to fix his mistake and redeem himself. For instance, if the player misses a dig, then the instructor can attack a ball at him in the same fashion. If the player attacks a ball out of bounds, the instructor can toss a ball that he has to attack. Players get one or two chances to fix errors; when they do, play continues with the appropriate number of contacts that the side has left. If the player can't fix the mistake with one or two redemption opportunities, he is replaced by a waiting player.

TO INCREASE DIFFICULTY

- Make the redemption opportunity more challenging.
- Require a push-up or squat jump between redemption opportunities.

TO DECREASE DIFFICULTY

- Allow players to make two or more errors, but not the same type of error twice.

Success Check

- Take an aggressive crescendo approach.
- Aim for the greatest amount of available court on the opponent's side.
- Swing with confidence.

Score Your Success

Play out the entire game (never replaced) = 10 points

Replaced once = 5 points

Your score ___

Variation Drill 4 **Coed and Reverse Coed**

Use the rules of coed and reverse coed volleyball and play a tournament. Play a game to 25 points. Teams that are off act as officials, scorekeepers, and line judges to practice what it would be like at a recreational tournament.

TO INCREASE DIFFICULTY

- Have the officiating teams call the set as if it were a championship (tightly with little room for error).

TO DECREASE DIFFICULTY

- Let the players play without making a lot of calls.

(continued)

Variation Drill 4 *(continued)*

Success Check

- Start in your top rotation.
- Discuss the roles for which each player is best suited.

Score Your Success

Win the set = 10 points

Score 15 to 23 points = 5 points

Score 14 or fewer points = 1 point

Your score ____

Variation Drill 5　Sitting Volleyball

Lower the net and use painter's tape to create a smaller court. Play a set to 25 points of sitting volleyball according the rules outlined in this step.

TO INCREASE DIFFICULTY

- Apply the U-S-A drill approach to the game.

TO DECREASE DIFFICULTY

- Provide redemption opportunities to players who make errors and continue play.

Success Check

- Make passes high enough that teammates have time to get to the ball.
- Serve tough to gain an early advantage.
- Don't forget to block!

Score Your Success

Win the set = 10 points

Score 15 to 23 points = 5 points

Score 14 or fewer points = 1 point

Your score ____

Variation Drill 6　Wallyball

Move your practice to a Wallyball court and practice your volleyball skills in a new environment. How can you gain an advantage the quickest while others are getting accustomed to the rule and environment changes? Play two or three sets to 15 points.

TO INCREASE DIFFICULTY

- Use side-out scoring entirely.

TO DECREASE DIFFICULTY

- Use normal volleyball scoring to simplify.

Success Check

- Use the walls to your advantage.
- Control the ball on your side of the net.
- Be ready to block or attack the serve. You can't do that in volleyball!

Score Your Success

Win two sets = 10 points

Win one set = 5 points

Win no sets = 1 point

Your score ___

Variation Drill 7　Original Volleyball Rules

Use Morgan's original rules from 1897 to play volleyball. Team A starts with the serve to initiate play. If team A wins the rally, they receive the point. If team B wins the rally, then team A receives an out. When team A gets three outs, the serve goes to team B and they follow suit. When team B gets three outs, both teams rotate and the serve returns to team A. After nine innings, the team with more points wins.

TO INCREASE DIFFICULTY

- Give teams fewer outs.

TO DECREASE DIFFICULTY

- Give teams more outs and chances to score.

Success Check

- Because it is guaranteed that you will get through all rotations, look for matchup advantages over starting your best rotation early.
- Play hard start to finish.

Score Your Success

Your team wins the game = 10 points

The other team wins the game = 5 points

Your score ___

Variation Drill 8　Side-Out vs. Rally Scoring

Play a game to 7 points with rotation and serve in rally-scoring format. With the same teams, start over at 0 and use side-out scoring (you score a point only if you have the serve). Did one game take longer than the other? What skills received greater emphasis in each format?

TO INCREASE DIFFICULTY

- Play to 15 points instead of 7.

TO DECREASE DIFFICULTY

- Provide a redemption opportunity and the chance to correct an error.

(continued)

Variation Drill 8 *(continued)*

Success Check

- Inside-out scoring, you can be more aggressive with your serve. Go after it!
- Start with your top rotations early in the match.

Score Your Success

Your team wins the game (rally scoring) = 10 points

The other team wins the game (rally scoring) = 5 points

Your team wins the game (side-out scoring) = 10 points

The other team wins the game (rally scoring) = 5 points

Your score ___

SUCCESS SUMMARY

With so many volleyball venues and formats, you will have ample opportunity to put your newfound skills to good use. Whether you take your game to the beach or to a racquetball court, a grass tournament or a reverse coed indoor league, remember to execute your skills with control and discipline, but don't be afraid to make mistakes. Errors are a part of the game, and as long as you continue to learn and grow from them you will continue to step further and further on your own. Because it is impossible to compete in volleyball alone, every time you play comes with it the opportunity to influence the enjoyment of others' experience. Make the most of it by modeling a positive attitude, relentless effort, and supportive environment. It will influence not only their enjoyment of the experience, but their success as well. I wish you all the best. Keep climbing!

Variation Drills

1.	Split-court doubles	___out of 10
2.	Speedball	___out of 10
3.	Redemption	___out of 10
4.	Coed and reverse coed	___out of 10
5.	Sitting volleyball	___out of 10
6.	Wallyball	___out of 10
7.	Original volleyball rules	___out of 10
8.	Side-out vs. rally scoring	___out of 20
	Total	**___out of 90**

Glossary

ace—any serve that contacts the floor or results in an unplayable contact by the opponent and results in a point for the serving team.

ball-handling error—in the judgment of the first referee, any illegal contact while playing the ball.

block—any contact by the defensive team of an attacked ball higher than the net and in front of the 10-foot (3m) line that results in the ball returning to the offensive side of the net.

block assist—a block that results in a point and involves two players jumping.

block touch—any contact by the defensive team of an attacked ball higher than the net and in front of the 10-foot (3m) line.

bunch blocking—a defensive strategy to move the base position of pin blockers toward the middle blocker in order to facilitate double blocking the middle attack.

collapse dig—defensive passing technique to position the platform under a ball attacked directly in front of the defense player.

crescendo approach—the footwork used when attacking that demonstrates a movement from slow to fast, small to big.

dig—any defensive contact of an attacked ball that continues a rally.

dive—an emergency defensive technique involving the sprawling effort of a player to keep the ball off the ground by lunging for the ground.

double block—when two front-row players jump side by side and put their hands above the height of the net into the path of an oncoming attack.

double contact—an illegal contact in which the ball touches two different body parts in succession.

dump—when the second contact is attacked, usually by surprise by the setter.

end line—the back line of the court, also referred to as the service line.

error—on a statistical box score, refers to any attacking attempt that results in a point for the other team (e.g., goes out of bounds or into the net, is blocked to the floor by the opponent, is illegally contacted, or involves illegal contact with the net).

first referee—the official who has final authority, stands in an elevated position, and is responsible for managing the pace of the game and judging all player contacts.

five-passer system—a serve-receive arrangement that allocates court coverage responsibility to every player (usually in the shape of a W).

joust—the effort a front-row player makes to play a ball that is in the plane of the net and can be attacked by both teams.

jump float serve—a serve contacted by a server who has left the ground; it has very little spin, causing the ball to veer from the passer in unpredictable ways.

jump set—an overhead pass to an attacker in which the player leaves the ground.

jump spin serve—a serve that is contacted by a server who has left the ground and forcefully throws his or her hand over the top of the ball to create spin.

kill—an attack that results in a point.

left-side hitter—the player who moves to zone 4 of the court for a base position and is often the easiest player on the court to set.

libero—a designated defensive specialist who has the flexibility to go in for any back-row player and does not have to go through subbing protocols, but cannot attack above the height of the net or set an attack in front of the 10-foot (3 m) line.

line judge—a member of the officiating team who identifies balls as in or out of bounds while also looking for touches by the defensive team.

man-back (perimeter) defense—a defensive system in which the player positioned in zone 6 stays deep to cover the end line. It is also referred to as a read defense because players have flexibility to move to places on the court that they believe the opponent will attack.

overhead pass—a way to play the ball with two hands above the forehead.

pass—any contact made on a ball that is not attacked with the forearms or hands.

pin blocker—a front-row blocker on either the right or left side of the court close to the antenna (pin).

platform—what is created when a passer aligns the thumbs, extends the elbows, and brings the forearms together.

quick set—a short set directly to the height of the contact point of the approaching hitter's arm swing.

rally scoring—a scoring system that allocates a point to the winner of every rally regardless of serve.

red card—a misconduct penalty resulting in a point given by an official for repeated violations of protocol or unsportsmanlike conduct. Repeated red cards can result in the expulsion of a player or coach.

replay—when a rally needs to be repeated to protect the safety of players (e.g., a ball from another court rolls on) or because of a disputed rally and officials are unsure of the correct call.

roll shot—an off-speed attack that is contacted with the palm of the hand and arched over the block, usually to a shallow location in the opponent's court.

rotation defense—a defensive system in which the player positioned in zone 6 moves to the sideline to dig against an outside hitter and the sideline digger defends the tip.

second referee—the official who stands on the bench side of the net across from the first referee and is primarily responsible for identifying net and center-line violations and overlaps in rotational positioning and communicating with the scorer's table.

service error—any errant serve that goes out of bounds or into the net, crosses the end line before contact, or is illegally contacted (e.g., lift or double contact).

set—an overhead pass to an attacker.

side-out scoring—a scoring system seldom used in the modern game, requiring a team to win the rally while they possess the serve to earn a point. Side-out games were generally played to 15 points.

soft block—an attempt by a shorter blocker to slow or redirect an attacked ball up so that it can be dug more easily by the defense. This is achieved by tilting the hands back (palms facing the ceiling) instead of reaching over the net to block the attack to the opponent's court.

speaking captain—the player designated to communicate with the first referee.

spread blocking—a blocking strategy that keeps the pin blockers closer to the antenna. This prevents them from helping as blockers on middle attacks but ensures that they are in a position to block the outside attackers at the pins.

standing float serve—a serve in which the server stays on the ground and holds the palm to the target following contact, limiting the spin on the ball and causing it to veer unpredictably as it travels to the opponent.

standing spin serve—a serve that is contacted by a server who is standing on the ground and forcefully throws the hand over the top of the ball to create spin.

solo block—a block by a single player that results in a point.

swing blocking—a blocking technique that uses an approach and arm swing similar to attacking.

three-passer system—when three players are positioned in a serve-reception pattern and each one passes the balls served into their third of the court.

triple block—a block that results in a point when three players have jumped.

two-passer system—when two players are positioned in a serve-reception pattern and each one passes the balls served into their half of the court.

yellow card—a misconduct penalty given by an official as a warning for violations of protocol or unsportsmanlike conduct.

About the Author

Becky Schmidt has made her mark on Hope College volleyball as both a player and head coach, a position she has held since 2004. The 2014 Flying Dutch won more than 20 matches for the 10th consecutive season, culminating in the school's first-ever NCAA DIII National Championship.

Having coached at both Hope and University of Redlands in California, Schmidt has a winning percentage of .762, ranking her among the nation's elite coaches. She has twice guided the Flying Dutch to undefeated seasons (16-0) in Michigan Intercollegiate Athletic Association (MIAA) conference play (2005 and 2009). Her 2009 team set a school record of winning 34 matches, a mark equaled in 2014.

In 2008, Schmidt was elected the NCAA Division III representative to the American Volleyball Coaches Association (AVCA) board of directors. Schmidt is a 1999 graduate of Hope College, where as a middle blocker she was twice voted MIAA Conference's Most Valuable Player. During her senior year she became the first Hope volleyball player to earn All-American honors.

Schmidt was a graduate assistant volleyball coach at Miami University of Ohio, where she earned her master's degree in sport behavior and performance. She has coached club volleyball teams in Michigan, Ohio, and California, and in 2002 she coached a USA Athletes International team to a gold medal in Australia's Down Under Games.

Schmidt lives in Holland, Michigan.

STEPS TO SUCCESS SPORTS SERIES

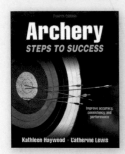

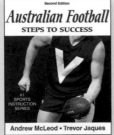

The *Steps to Success Sports Series* is the most extensively researched and carefully developed set of books ever published for teaching and learning sports skills.

Each of the books offers a complete progression of skills, concepts, and strategies that are carefully sequenced to optimize learning for students, teaching for sport-specific instructors, and instructional program design techniques for future teachers.

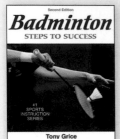 Badminton — Tony Grice

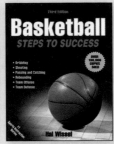 Basketball — Hal Wissel

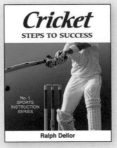 Bowling — Doug Wiedman

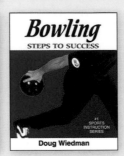 Cricket — Ralph Dellor

 Fencing — Elaine Cheris

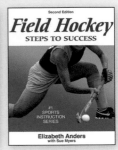 Field Hockey — Elizabeth Anders with Sue Myers

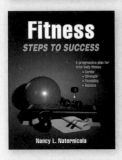 Fitness — Nancy L. Naternicola

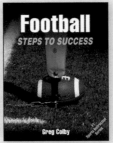 Football — Greg Colby

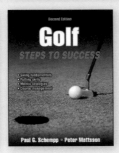 Golf — Paul G. Schempp • Peter Mattsson

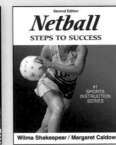 Ice Skating — Karin Künzle-Watson, Stephen J. DeArmond

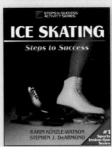 Netball — Wilma Shakespear / Margaret Caldow

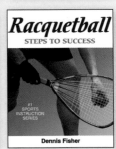 Racquetball — Dennis Fisher

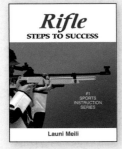 Rifle — Launi Meili

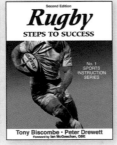 Rugby — Tony Biscombe • Peter Drewett, Foreword by Ian McGeechan, OBE

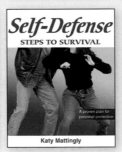 Self-Defense — Katy Mattingly

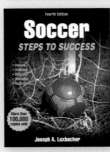 Soccer — Joseph A. Luxbacher

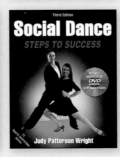 Social Dance — Judy Patterson Wright

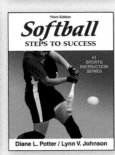 Softball — Diane L. Potter / Lynn V. Johnson

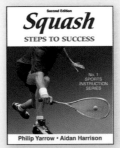 Squash — Philip Yarrow • Aidan Harrison

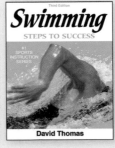 Swimming — David Thomas

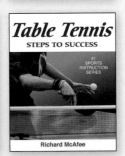 Table Tennis — Richard McAfee

 Tennis — Jim Brown • Camille Soullor

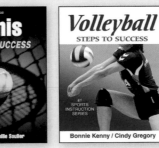 Volleyball — Bonnie Kenny / Cindy Gregory

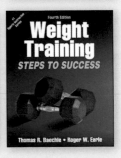 Weight Training — Thomas R. Baechle • Roger W. Earle

To place your order, U.S. customers call
TOLL FREE **1-800-747-4457**
In Canada call 1-800-465-7301
In Australia call 08 8372 0999
In Europe call +44 (0) 113 255 5665
In New Zealand call 0800 222 062
or visit **www.HumanKinetics.com/StepstoSuccess**

HUMAN KINETICS
The Premier Publisher for Sports & Fitness
P.O. Box 5076, Champaign, IL 61825-5076